G000279148

"If it's true that what we chase [...]
see the world around us really [...]
is a much-needed resource that directs the way we engage
with culture as women of God, and I'm grateful to these
sisters for lending their wisdom—for such a time as this."

RUTH CHOU SIMONS, Author, *GraceLaced* and
***Beholding and Becoming*; Founder, gracelaced.com**

"For the busy woman who wants to engage and live a life of
biblical significance but feels unprepared, this book is for you!
Trillia Newbell has done a wonderful job of recruiting women
who can help us evaluate culture and articulate biblical truth
as we learn to think, listen and speak to a world that in many
ways has lost its mooring. Anchored in Scripture, this book
will be a tool you will reference often. No more retreating: it is
time for us to engage and be *beautifully distinct!*"

DONNA GAINES, Editor, *A Daily Women's Devotional*;
Founder and President, ARISE2Read

"The women who have written in this book know what it
means to be in this world but not of it. Through their thoughtful reflections, they demonstrate how our salvation changes
not just us, but also the way we relate to the culture around us.
These are women I respect and feel privileged to learn from."

AMY WHITFIELD, SBC Executive Committee; Associate
Vice President, Convention Communications

"*Beautifully Distinct* is an important resource on culture
written by Christian women. These authors bring a helpful
perspective as they consider how being a disciple of Jesus
Christ affects every area of our lives. Their insights will
challenge and encourage every reader."

PHILLIP BETHANCOURT, Executive Vice President,
Ethics & Religious Liberty Commission

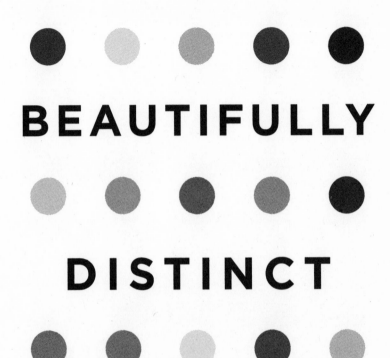

BEAUTIFULLY

DISTINCT

CONVERSATIONS WITH FRIENDS ON FAITH, LIFE, AND CULTURE

 ERLC

Beautifully Distinct
© ERLC 2020

Published by:
The Good Book Company

thegoodbook.com | thegoodbook.co.uk
thegoodbook.com.au | thegoodbook.co.nz | thegoodbook.co.in

Unless otherwise indicated, Scripture quotations are from The Holy Bible, English
Standard Version (ESV), copyright © 2001 by Crossway, a publishing ministry of
Good News Publishers. Used by permission. All rights reserved.

All rights reserved. Except as may be permitted by the Copyright Act, no part of
this publication may be reproduced in any form or by any means without prior
permission from the publisher.

The ERLC has asserted its right under the Copyright, Designs and Patents Act 1988
to be identified as author of this work.

ISBN: 9781784985219 | Printed in Denmark

Design by André Parker

CONTENTS

INTRODUCTION

TRILLIA NEWBELL

It's amazing when you see God making a noticeable difference in your life. When I first became a Christian, I was thrilled about Jesus but didn't fully understand what my new profession of faith meant for how I related to the rest of the world around me. So every time I saw something new in God's word, light bulbs went off in my head about how that one fact should change the way I lived.

In the first few pages of Genesis I found that humans are made in the image of God. Since that's the case, it matters how we treat those not like us; it matters how we think about and relate to the opposite sex; it matters how we treat the immigrant. That one fact transformed my worldview and how I would then live in the world. That's only one! What would happen as I read the rest of what God had to say?

As Jesus said when he prayed for his disciples in John 17, we are being "sanctified in truth"—transformed to think and live God's way (v 19). That is what I was experiencing as I started to read God's word. It was changing me from the inside out.

Being sanctified in truth means that we become beautifully distinct from the rest of the world. We are given a new identity in Christ and set apart from the world. We no longer think and live as the world thinks and lives, but as God commands. And this can be compelling and attractive.

Even though I've now been a Christian for many years, I'm still continually evaluating what the world tells me and weighing it against God's word. But there are so many messages—from the government, from the internet, from our neighbors, from our family, from the TV—that this can be very difficult. What should I think about this issue or that news story? Who should I talk to and what should I say? What should I eat? What should I wear? What should I watch or read?

All of these questions can make being beautifully distinct seem unattainable. You may be confused by all the world's instructions for living. Or maybe your life is so full that you don't have time to stop and properly consider what is influencing you. Or maybe you are afraid of what others might think as you attempt to put your faith into action.

Here's the good news: our salvation really does change everything about us. Peter writes, "But you are a chosen race, a royal priesthood, a holy nation, a people for his own possession, that you may proclaim the excellencies of him who called you out of darkness into his marvelous light" (1 Peter 2 v 9). This is who we are, and this is what Jesus has sent us into the world to do. Thankfully, Peter is addressing us as the church, not just as individuals. We are a people belonging to God, so we can help each other to fulfill the wonderful task of proclaiming him to the world. That proclamation is in both word and deed.

More good news: we aren't walking alone. It's not only that we have each other, important though that is. If Jesus sent us into the world, he isn't then going to leave us to our own devices. He is still praying for us (Hebrews 7 v 25).

In John 17, the same passage where Jesus asks the Father to sanctify believers, he expresses his desire for us to live in the world proclaiming the truth we have been given. Jesus prays:

I have given them your word, and the world has hated them because they are not of the world, just as I am not of the world. I do not ask that you take them out of the world, but that you keep them from the evil one. They are not of the world, just as I am not of the world. Sanctify them in the truth; your word is truth. As you sent me into the world, so I have sent them into the world. (v 14-18)

Jesus doesn't mince words here—the world will not be our friend. Instead he says the world will hate us as it hates him. That doesn't mean we need to retreat, nor does it mean we need to grow cynical; instead we need to be ready. Jesus prays for that too. He says that he is sending us into the world. As we've seen, he prays that we would be sanctified and that this would be a result of us knowing his word. And as we go "into the world"—as we live and speak in a distinctive way—we will find that even in a world that rejects Jesus, many people will come to know and love Jesus as their Lord and Savior.

So we pray: Teach us your word, Lord, so we can walk in it!

Beautifully Distinct contains a series of short chapters meant to help us navigate many different areas of life and culture. It won't provide all the answers, but it will be a helpful guide for us on our quest to be sanctified by truth. This is the beginning of a conversation meant to get you and me thinking and asking questions as we engage the culture around us. Have you considered how what you read affects what you believe? What about the movies you watch? Who have you had in your home lately? Is there a way for you to communicate your own story compellingly for the Lord to use for his glory and the good of others? These are a few of the topics we'll address.

The first part of the book looks at five areas of everyday life, highlighting some of the messages and influences we meet in our culture on a regular basis, and encouraging us to be thoughtful about what we hear. We don't want to merely absorb the teachings of our age as we go into the world. If there are messages all around us—and there are—we need to be diligent in weighing what we hear by the word of God, which is what God uses to sanctify us.

A different temptation might be to retreat from the world and never expose ourselves to those things that seem counter to our Christian beliefs and morals. But God hasn't called us to an insular life, comfortably tucked away in our own homes and churches. He has sent us into the world. Jesus reminds us in John 17 v 15 that we have the protection of a good and holy God, who can "keep [us] from the evil one." So we don't need to be afraid. Instead we have the opportunity to listen to those who are not like us, reaching out and seeking to understand new perspectives so that we can go "into the world" effectively with the message of Jesus. This is what the second part of this book is designed to help with.

The final three chapters consider ways of speaking well for Christ, proclaiming the truth about him in a way that can change your community. In a world where words are many, you and I will want to be cautious about how we speak. Our opinions can be shared at the click of a button and go out to hundreds or thousands within seconds. We ought not to be overly hasty in speaking out against the voices we don't like. Instead, the thoughts and opinions we share should be said out of love, covered in prayer, and backed by Scripture. Our ultimate goal is to share the message of Jesus.

Every chapter is insightful, biblical, and practical. Each one will encourage and equip you to be beautifully distinct as you engage the culture around you—all for the sake of the Lord Jesus. So, pull up a seat and make yourself comfortable. Maybe grab a friend or two to have this conversation with you.

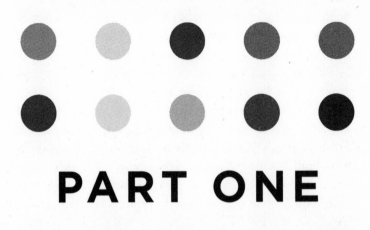

PART ONE

BEING THOUGHTFUL

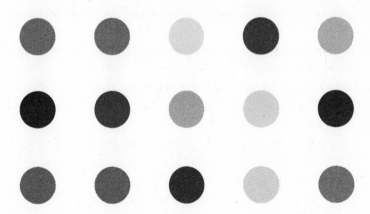

BEING THOUGHTFUL:

INTRODUCTION TO PART 1

ALISSA WILKINSON AND
KAREN SWALLOW PRIOR

We want to say to women: your voice is needed.

Do you ever think about how unique each person's perspective is? When you watch a film, you don't watch it as anyone else. You watch it as you, and you respond to it as you. Every person has their own thoughts and opinions and voice.

But women's voices can be few and far between. As a teacher of criticism, I (Alissa) have found that it is often young women, more than the men who come through my class, who are really good at what they are doing. Yet, in three years as a film critic at *Christianity Today*, I have received only two pitches from women writers, while I might get two a day from men.

There aren't a lot of women in criticism. Maybe we feel that we are not allowed to be there. When I wrote a startled tweet about the pitches in my inbox, several women said to me, "We didn't know we were allowed to ask."

The perspectives of women are different from those of men. We need to speak up. We don't all have to be professional critics, but we do all have to be critics. We have to engage with culture.

"Culture" could be considered as things humans make in order to make sense of the world. We all do that. We all consume culture, accepting its narratives and passing them on. This means that women have a vital role to play in the shaping of culture, whether or not they are professional critics. We influence the other people in our lives. We are often the ones who decide what our children watch and play and eat and hear about. We are the ones who show them who they are and where they are going and what life is about.

But oftentimes we are just not thinking about all this. We don't take a proactive role in shaping the culture of our families and communities. We accept what we hear and see and read without really considering it or the way it changes our culture.

The word "criticism" can seem scary, so here's a synonym for you: thoughtful. Be thoughtful about whatever cultural phenomenon you are engaging with. The biggest thing any of us can do when it comes to culture is to experience it and then to talk about it with other people thoughtfully. We should encourage each other to consider what we really think and what kinds of things we want to promote in our community.

What do I think about how much time my family spends looking at our phones? How are the narratives of sappy rom-coms or best-selling novels influencing me? What should I say to my friends about the latest hit TV series? Why is it that my kids want a particular video game, and how could I meet their needs in a better way?

We may not know the answers to all these questions, but as Christian women we can start by considering each cultural phenomenon in the light of the Bible and asking for God's help as we seek to practice discernment. We shouldn't retreat from the world and from secular culture; nor should we embrace everything in it. We need to strive for a third way, informed by both truth and love, both grace and law (see Matthew 5 v 17-20; Romans 5 v 20-21).

The chapters in this section are examples of how to listen thoughtfully to the culture around us in this way. Each one takes a different sphere, highlights some of the narratives we may hear there, and helps us to think more carefully about them. Thinking critically about the movies, games, food, books, advertisements, and TV shows that we and our families enjoy every day will help us to start to see how we can shape our culture—and shape it for Christ.

1. MOVIES: SPEAKING OUR CULTURE'S LANGUAGE

CATHERINE PARKS

When I was in college, I joined a "Worldview Team." We went around to Christian high schools and youth groups, teaching kids to "think worldviewishly"—to examine the messages of pop culture and identify the true and false ideas present in them. We asked questions about the movies they saw and the music they listened to: What idea of God does the artist present? Is man mostly good or mostly bad? Is life given purpose and meaning, or is it random and meaningless? Is there absolute truth, or do we determine our own truth? We would play clips of Eminem songs and movies like *Serendipity* and *Bruce Almighty* (I'm aging myself a bit here), unpacking the ideas they contained and discussing the way they presented religion.

Some kids resisted this. Their faces said, "You're just trying to tell me I can't enjoy this."

But that wasn't our purpose.

In our current age, film and TV are the means of visual storytelling with which we are most familiar. Movies and TV shows are our cultural language. We communicate through easily recognizable GIFs of famous moments and pictures of celebrities. Film quotes serve as immediate connecting points with strangers. I can see a movie, post about it on social media, and immediately have conversations with people around the world who have also seen it. These visual stories are woven into the fabric of our society, and they change us in ways we don't always notice.

Our Worldview Team wasn't about trying to tell those kids not to enjoy movies. We wanted to help them keep their minds engaged as they enjoyed them, so that they wouldn't just blindly buy into whatever messages a movie contained.

Any of us can seek to develop this way of thinking and see what messages the movies we watch are giving us. As we do so, we'll enjoy popular culture more deeply, we'll make our viewing choices more wisely, we'll understand those around us more naturally, and we'll see the truth and beauty of God in places we never expected.

UNINTENDED MESSAGES

Sometimes teachers in the schools the Worldview Team visited would be concerned that we were showing the kids "secular" media. They seemed unaware that most of these kids were already listening to and watching these and many other things! They thought anything that wasn't explicitly Christian was unhealthy. But it doesn't take much to see that many "secular" movies contain surprisingly biblical messages.

I was in my twenties the first time I saw *E.T. the Extra-Terrestrial.* As soon as it was over, I looked at my husband in disbelief and told him I never knew it was so rich with Christological symbolism. This is the story of a being who comes to Earth, lives at first in an old shack, is welcomed and trusted by children, takes their sickness upon himself, dies, is resurrected, and then ascends back into the heavens. Does this sound familiar? Even unbelievers have recognized the film's religious symbolism.

Director Steven Spielberg has insisted he did not set out to make E.T. a Christ figure. His Jewish background would make such a mission unlikely. Yet it's hard even for him to deny that the messages are present in the film. In a 1982 interview in *LA Weekly*, he responded to questions about religious symbolism in another of his films simply by saying, "I've been too busy making movies to stop and analyze how or why I make 'em."

It's possible that Melissa Mathison, *E.T.*'s screenwriter, did intend to write a New Testament allegory. There are mixed reports. But if she did, Spielberg never noticed. We can take an artist's words about his or her intended message into account, but it's also possible to see meanings in movies and other media that have found their way in without the artist realizing it: meanings that can include a grand-scale view of God.

SUBTLE LIES

Of course, there are also subtle messages that have more harmful effects. The teachers at those schools we visited were worried about "secular" media, and it's true that some content is harmful and inappropriate. It may tempt us to lust, for example, or trigger fear or anxiety. It's important to exercise discernment in choosing what to watch. There are plenty of online resources to help us evaluate this, such as reviews and content advisories.

But sometimes the most harmful content is not overt. Movies can contain subtle lies which change the way we think or the expectations we have for our lives.

One example is found in many of the romantic comedies I watched in college. It may seem too much to say that such silly and unrealistic movies have some large worldview message. Of course I never for a moment thought I would meet the love of my life when my heel got caught in a manhole cover or someone came to interview me about my inability to follow through on wedding plans. Yet there was an overall message which I did absorb. It was natural when watching these films to think the most important thing in life was romantic love. If only I met the right person, in the right way, my life would be better.

I would never have actually said this, nor did I think I believed it. But in the same way that breathing in carbon monoxide can poison you without you ever knowing it, so immersing ourselves in harmful, untruthful stories can sell us a lie we might never notice. Watching all those romantic comedies in college gave me wrong ideas about my life and what I should be prioritizing. It was only when I started to really think about their messages that I realized it.

Sometimes even so-called Christian movies present subtle lies. If our presentation of the Christian life is one in which all problems are solved easily and immediately, we are not telling the truth about the "already/not yet" reality in which we live our lives. While we should acknowledge God's power and ability to work in any situation, these fairy tale-like endings will ring false to those who are walking through suffering that doesn't seem to be resolved so easily. We should create and support Christian art that is honest about the true nature of God's grace and the cross-bearing life we're called to.

MEANINGFUL CONVERSATIONS

But understanding the messages in the movies or TV shows we watch isn't just about practicing discernment for our own sakes. We are also being equipped to listen to and love the people around us.

This is partly because movies can show us what it feels like to go through things we will never experience for ourselves. Sitting in a theater and watching actors depict joy and suffering gives me a small taste of understanding of the type of person or situation being portrayed. It's often the closest thing to what Harper Lee's Atticus Finch said in *To Kill a Mockingbird*: "You never really understand a person until you consider things from his point of view ... Until you climb into his skin and walk around in it." Movies give us the opportunity to experience the pain and joy of our neighbors and fellow image-bearers around the world. They create empathy in us for other people.

In addition, when we engage our minds about something that people around us are watching, we understand the messages they are buying into. Because visual media are such an important part of our cultural context, thinking about movies gives us the opportunity to speak the cultural language. It's an entry point for meaningful conversation. Our ability to sort through the messages and emotions of a movie or TV show allows us to diagnose the spiritual needs not only of its creators but also of our fellow consumers.

Noticing the impact romantic comedies had on me has made me better able to understand my friends who watch lots of those movies too. I can think about why they love them and what messages and stories they are seeking to hear. I can challenge what they believe about themselves and what they are expecting for their romantic relationships. I can suggest other things to watch or listen to that would contain messages which tell them the truth instead of those subtle lies.

Film critic Josh Larsen goes so far as to say that movies are prayers.[1] Not in the sense that they are explicitly intended to speak to God, of course, but in the sense that they are a means of expressing human emotions: gratitude, lament, regret, fear, or joy. Just as the psalmists directed these emotions to God in their songs, today directors, screenwriters and actors express their emotions in movies, directing their deepest feelings outside themselves as if to a higher power.

Perhaps the artist is expressing a lament about the brokenness in the world or a longing for a better home.

Maybe it's a desire for deep, soul-satisfying love sought in the wrong people and places. Or when an artist depicts incredible feats of strength or talent, it could lead us to praise God for the amazing gifts given to those who bear God's image. The visual arts give us a means of expressing our deepest feelings, fears, and joys, even if we don't realize to whom we are expressing them.

This observation that movies are like prayers is not so different from Paul's statement when he preached in Athens: "Men of Athens, I perceive that in every way you are very religious" (Acts 17 v 22). As Paul walked around Athens, he realized the Athenians were reaching out to the true God without really knowing him. Among the many idols he saw, he found one with an inscription that read "To the unknown god." Paul told them, "What therefore you worship as unknown, this I proclaim to you" (Acts 17 v 23). He went on to give them the answer they needed: that the God who created them can be known.

When we seek to understand the messages in the movies we and our friends are watching, we are giving ourselves the tools to have a similar conversation—identifying the desires and longings of people's hearts, and showing them how these are met in Christ.

GOOD QUESTIONS

Learning to identify these feelings and longings has been a helpful tool to use with my children. Sometimes after watching something together, I will ask them what they thought certain characters were feeling at different points in the movie. A simple conversation like this conveys to them that the emotions they feel are normal and part of the way God designed them. It opens the door for us to identify ways in which characters expressed their emotions and whether those were healthy expressions or not.

Similarly, my husband, Erik, is great about asking our kids to identify symbolism and the messages of a movie, training them to view the story with their minds engaged. And it's not just to our kids that he asks these questions. For several years he has hosted occasional "Manly Movie Nights," which began with stereotypically masculine movies like *Braveheart* and *Warrior* and now include obscure Belgian films and dark Irish dramedies. At first when he began a conversation after the movie, it was awkwardly silent. Like strengthening an unused muscle, learning to look more deeply at movies takes time, and doing it collectively can feel strange. But Erik and his friends—both believers and nonbelievers—have learned so much from each other through this simple practice of asking questions about symbols, messages, themes, longing, and worldviews.

And it should come as no surprise that using stories can be an excellent entry point for gospel conversations, since this is just what Jesus did in his teaching ministry. How often did he illustrate truth with a story that his listeners could relate to? We may not be the ones telling the stories, but we can pray for discernment and wisdom to connect the stories we hear and see with the truth we know. This happens most often when we ask good questions like "Did you connect with any of the characters?" or "How did you feel while watching that?" or even something as simple as "What did you think about that movie?" Asking that question, and then listening intently to the response, can open our eyes to the views and ideals of the people around us.

None of this wisdom, insight and discernment are possible, however, unless we have in place a framework within which to view movies and TV. It is when we have tasted and seen the goodness of the Lord in the truth of his word that we are able to realize that other tastes and sights can never truly satisfy. Those who don't know this are at the mercy of the messages they hear in the culture around them.

Engaging with movies means that we can understand a major way in which people in our culture express themselves and might reach out to God without even knowing it. We understand what they believe and what they are living for. We, who know the truth about what God is like and how to reach him, must make sure we are part of that conversation.

2. WHEN FOOD BECOMES
A FALSE GOSPEL

KELLY NEEDHAM

In 2004, the documentary *Supersize Me* birthed a movement of fear-based eating. Though it's unlikely that many folks had ever actually thought it wise to exclusively eat at McDonalds, Morgan Spurlock struck fear in the hearts of anyone who'd ever purchased a Happy Meal.

Many food-based documentaries have since been released into our living rooms, sharing one key feature: fear of certain foods. Sugar. GMOs. Preservatives. Gluten. Corn. This information overload has turned a simple trip to the grocery store into a dance through a minefield. You'd better have done your research so you can avoid the hidden toxins lurking in each ingredient list!

This growing food-fear raises a question: what can save us from these hazards? Each documentary (and blogger, and nutritionist, and neighbor) answers differently. Supplements. Organic. Paleo. Vitamins. Gluten-free. Cleanses. Vegan. Gut health. Essential Oils. Ketones. If you don't choose a solution, it can feel as though you've just conceded: you're letting "the industry" kill off your family with cancer, high cholesterol or obesity.

So should I do the Whole30 diet? The Daniel Fast? (Isn't that biblical?) Gluten-free or dairy-free? Which one is right? Is cancer really right around the corner for me if I eat preservative-rich food? Will my irritability and laziness really decrease if I cut out sugar?

It's worth noting that all these options and opinions are only possible in a culture of abundance. In countries where food is scarce and poverty is rampant, you take what you can get. Options are a privilege of the wealthy. We worry about what we *should* eat because we don't have to worry that we *will* eat.

Instead of casting around for the right fad diet, we should remember that the Bible speaks authoritatively to every generation in every culture in every age, no matter whether that culture is poor or rich, and regardless of what foods they like to eat. Thankfully, God has plenty to say about food in the Bible. And his Spirit-breathed word is just as applicable today as when the words were penned on parchment.

These questions may seem to have little to do with God, but in fact they are utterly theological. How we understand God and the gospel should inform the way we think about food and help us have a wise approach to health-food documentaries, advertising campaigns, and supermarket aisles.

WHEN FOOD BECOMES A FALSE GOSPEL

And do not fear those who kill the body but cannot kill the soul. Rather fear him who can destroy both soul and body in hell. (Matthew 10 v 28)

Jesus speaks in this verse to our fear of what can kill the body. He doesn't deny that the threat of death is real but tells us that our fear is shortsighted. We face a greater, eternal danger. Why does this matter? Because what we fear directs where we put our faith.

The day-to-day reality for most of us is not the fear of being killed. Instead we give way to countless other temporal fears which blind us to the eternal perspective, driving us to put our faith in something other than Jesus.

If we fear weight gain, we'll trust in foods that promote weight loss. If we fear cravings, we'll trust in foods known to stifle appetite. If we fear GMOs, we'll trust in foods that boast of all-natural ingredients.

Now, I don't want to imply that health food is bad. We all know we should eat a balanced diet and exercise well. It's wise to look after our bodies properly. For some, a particular diet is actually a health requirement—if you have an intolerance or you suffer from a disease which affects your digestive system, you have to be careful about what you eat. For many who suffer in this way or who look after others who do, a great deal of care, wisdom, and effort is required to complete what for the rest of us is just a simple trip to the grocery store.

Being wise and careful about food is good. But there is a difference between being wise and careful and putting all your hopes into your diet. The danger is that our health food of choice can become a functional savior. It's as if healthy eating is a new gospel. But in truth it is no gospel at all. It focuses on the temporal, not the eternal. By shining the spotlight on the food in front of us, it keeps heaven and hell on the back burner.

This false gospel also proposes Christ-less solutions to sin-based problems. Overeating, irritability, and cravings are sin problems to which Jesus alone is the solution. Like giving a flu shot to a cancer patient, giving any solution other than Christ to those sick with sin is futile at best and deceptive at worst. When we are irritable or ill-disciplined, we need to recognize that these sins come from within us, not from anything outside. Of course, some practical things do help us, like keeping chocolate bars out of the home to keep us from gluttony.

But real change comes from the power of the Spirit; it's his help we need to ask for. We need to look forward to the day when, thanks to Jesus, we will be fully free from sin at last.

Ours is not the first generation to put its fears and its hope in food. Paul wrote about this repeatedly, reminding the early churches that regulations about eating and drinking could become an enemy of the true gospel.

> If with Christ you died to the elemental spirits of the world, why, as if you were still alive in the world, do you submit to regulations—"Do not handle, Do not taste, Do not touch" (referring to things that all perish as they are used)—according to human precepts and teachings? (Colossians 2 v 20-22)

Following "human precepts and teachings" about eating and drinking does not just distract us from God by persuading us to focus on our temporal desires to feel good or look the right shape. It can also set itself up in opposition to the true gospel. In 1 Timothy 4 v 1-5, Paul's words are much stronger. Describing false teachers who, among other things, "require abstinence from foods," he says that they are departing from the faith "by devoting themselves to deceitful spirits and teachings of demons." The false gospel of health food subtly suggests that the abundant life and freedom from sin promised in Jesus can be found without going to Jesus himself.

The sad result of seeing health food as a savior is that we become evangelists for it, telling others about all the benefits, hoping to convince them that the cost, time, and inconvenience are worth it. We end up preaching a gospel that is—conveniently—far less offensive and far more easily shared with our neighbors than the gospel of Jesus Christ. Instead of helping them, we are distracting them from what is the real threat to their health: sin and its wages of death.

Christian, Jesus is your Savior, your freedom from sin, your promise of everlasting life. You already have good news to share and a charge to preach it to all the nations, convincing as many as possible that the cost of following Christ is worth it. Resist the urge to preach anything less.

HOW TO EAT TO GLORIFY GOD

At this point someone might well ask, "Does rejecting the health-food gospel mean I should give no thought to what I eat?" Of course not. The Bible speaks clearly about managing all that God has entrusted to us, including our bodies, in responsible, God-honoring ways (1 Corinthians 6 v 19-20). But that's not all that the Bible says about the issue. So how does the Bible instruct us to think about what we eat? Here are three ways to approach food to the glory of God.

1. EAT IN FAITH

Therefore do not be anxious, saying, "What shall we eat?" or "What shall we drink?" or "What shall we wear?" For the Gentiles seek after all these things, and your heavenly Father knows that you need them all. But seek first the kingdom of God and his righteousness, and all these things will be added to you. Therefore do not be anxious about tomorrow, for tomorrow will be anxious for itself. Sufficient for the day is its own trouble. (Matthew 6 v 31-34)

When my husband and I were in India to bring home our adopted son, the orphanage welcomed us with tea, muffins and cookies. The conditions for food preparation in this rural town were likely not ideal, and I knew the risks in eating and drinking what was offered. But I also knew how offensive it would be to reject this kindness. As representatives of Jesus in this foreign land, we ate in faith.

Faith that God could keep our bodies well, even when exposed to potential health risks.

I might not be in rural India anymore, but social media keeps me well aware of the potential health risks in the food we have here. And so I continue to eat in faith—faith that God sustains my body and can keep it in good health despite the hazards around me. This doesn't mean I lack common sense. Eating cheesecake three times a day probably isn't the best decision. But instead of over-analyzing all of our consumption—instead of worrying all the time about tomorrow—our family strives for a well-balanced diet according to the financial means God has provided. I trust God with any concerns that remain.

2. EAT TO SHARE THE GOSPEL

> *If one of the unbelievers invites you to dinner and you are disposed to go, eat whatever is set before you without raising any question on the ground of conscience ... So, whether you eat or drink, or whatever you do, do all to the glory of God ... just as I try to please everyone in everything I do, not seeking my own advantage, but that of many, that they may be saved.* (1 Corinthians 10 v 27, 31, 33)

Sharing a meal together has long been a basic form of human connection and, as such, a prime avenue for the gospel. Paul understood this. He tells us that gospel proclamation trumps food preference every time. Paul is talking about matters of conscience—his readers were concerned about whether or not to eat meat that had been sacrificed to idols. If his instruction even in that situation is to eat for the sake of the gospel, then it also applies to situations where it is only our preferences, not our consciences, that are at stake. We are to eat whatever is set before us without complaint, because the gospel is more important than a narrow palette or even our optimal health.

Now, if you are allergic to peanuts, by all means don't eat the PB&J offered by your unbelieving neighbor. But if you prefer gluten-free bread simply because you feel better eating gluten-free food, this is your opportunity to trust God with your physical body and lay aside your preferences. Don't make much of food: make much of God. As you receive the hospitality of your neighbor, you will have a much better opportunity to tell them of the hospitality of God in the gospel.

3. EAT TO ENJOY GOD

[God] humbled you and let you hunger and fed you with manna, which you did not know, nor did your fathers know, that he might make you know that man does not live by bread alone, but man lives by every word that comes from the mouth of the LORD.

(Deuteronomy 8 v 3)

Jesus was born in a town named Bethlehem, which means "house of bread." As a baby he was laid in a feeding trough. Later he called himself the bread of life. What might he be telling us? Simply this: God intends our eating to remind us of a greater reality. God made us with a need for food so that we might understand our need for him. He alone can satisfy us!

Food is a shadow, a picture, of what God is for us. It is not ultimate. When Jesus was going through his forty-day fast in the desert, the devil tempted him to break his fast by turning stones into bread. But Jesus knew that what truly sustained him was not food but the word of God (Matthew 4 v 4). The same can be true for us too. Let's not elevate food to a position that it was never meant to occupy.

Instead, we can use food to remind ourselves of all the good gifts that God has given us and the fact that he has provided for us eternally. When we are hungry, we can remember that God is the one who knows all our needs. When we eat—whether our bread is gluten-free or sourdough, multigrain or plain white, or even if we don't eat bread at all—we can thank God for sending Jesus, the bread of life.

THE MOST IMPORTANT THING

No matter what choices we make and what food we prefer, we should always be careful that we don't fall into the trap of following the false gospel of healthy eating. The most important thing in life isn't being healthy. The truth is that following Jesus can actually be hazardous to our health. As his followers, we are promised persecution and suffering. In some parts of the world, to choose Christ is to choose a shorter life. That kind of sacrifice makes our daily worries about what to eat seem very small.

In the end, all of us will get sick in this life. All of us will die. Our hope lies not in a more exhaustive knowledge of food or better choices at the grocery store but in a Savior who truly is making all things new.

> *The one who observes the day, observes it in honor of the Lord. The one who eats, eats in honor of the Lord, since he gives thanks to God, while the one who abstains, abstains in honor of the Lord and gives thanks to God. For none of us lives to himself, and none of us dies to himself. For if we live, we live to the Lord, and if we die, we die to the Lord. So then, whether we live or whether we die, we are the Lord's. (Romans 14 v 6-8)*

3. SEX AND
OUR BODIES

DANNAH GRESH

Sixteen percent of all American women have read *Fifty Shades of Grey*. And 16% of all Christian women have done so too.[1] The movie versions of the trilogy have grossed over $1.3 billion.

What does it say that a series celebrating masochism and male dominance over female bodies has found such an audience not among men but predominantly among women? How is it that words such as "submission," "master," and "bondage" are—as long as they are accompanied by whips and chains—considered by so many not only as acceptable but sexy?

This kind of attitude toward women's bodies has had a much more serious impact in other significant ways, especially in the form of sexual abuse. The last few years have seen women of all ages, races, and religions bravely arming themselves with nothing more than a hashtag and stepping up to tell their stories of sexual harassment and assault and to call abusers to account. That the #MeToo movement is necessary is tragic; that it has brought these crimes to light is good.

But we still need to talk about the way women's bodies are viewed not only by some men but by many women—many of us—too.

BODY SHAMING

In the US the average adult female body today is size 16, but the average model is much smaller. One of the most highly paid models in the world, Gisele, wears a size 4, which is consistent with industry norms. Add to this the hours of flaw-removing, cheek-bone-enhancing makeup application followed by fictitious Photoshop perfecting, and it is easy to see why the impact on our daughters can be devastating.

According to a study in pediatrics, about two-thirds of girls in the 5th to 12th grades said that fashion photography influences their vision of an ideal body, and about half said that such images made them want to lose weight.[2] After twenty years of working daily with teen girls, I have yet to find a young woman saturated in the output from today's fashion and beauty industries who actually feels lovely. It seems that the harder a girl focuses on the world's standards, the less confident she feels about her own body.

Some girls will respond by seeking to cover up the bodies they feel ashamed of, but most try their hardest to live up to these unattainable, unrealistic standards. They look for expensive products, watch video tutorials on makeup, and try to lose weight. When some part of their body finally looks the way they want, many will wear revealing clothing to show it off. Nudity seems to have become a way of projecting confidence: 54% of teens in one survey said they had sent a sext message, with almost a third of them stating that it was a nude or semi-nude photo. Exposing their bodies in this way, they may argue, makes them feel beautiful and sexy.[3]

Many Christians have responded by emphasizing modest dressing. They use slogans like "Modest is hottest" and try to impose rules about the appropriate length of a skirt or the tightness of a shirt. They are trying to keep girls safe from a culture that seems full of dangerous and unhelpful expectations about female bodies.

When I use the word "modesty" in my own work, I receive no small amount of correspondence accusing me of "body shaming". The very idea of modesty has become poisonous to some. Partly this is because they assume that we hide only what we are ashamed of—whereas, as *New York Times* best-selling author Wendy Shalit points out, modesty should really be "an impulse that protects what is precious and intimate."[4] But there is also a problem with the modesty movement. Although it seems to oppose the modern obsession with women's bodies and outward appearance, it actually promotes this obsession in a different way. We focus on what we can and cannot wear, limiting our definition of modesty to the physical. We apply rules about clothing without taking time to explain why we think those guidelines are helpful. The danger is that this becomes just another version of the idealized, objectified female body.

Instead we need to communicate a complete theology of body and beauty. We need to see our bodies as an integral and precious part of ourselves: something to be respected and looked after, not something to be ashamed of. At the same time, we need to stop thinking that beauty is all about the body.

ONE WHOLE PERSON

Do not let your adorning be external—the braiding of hair and the putting on of gold jewelry, or the clothing you wear—but let your adorning be the hidden person of the heart with the imperishable beauty of a gentle and quiet spirit, which in God's sight is very precious.
(1 Peter 3 v 3-4)

These verses encourage Christian women to cultivate true beauty, which has to do with our internal disposition. Peter begins by instructing us not to be obsessed with worldly standards of beauty. Instead we should focus on the heart.

God does not condemn physical beauty nor the expression of it. He continually adorns himself with things that we consider beautiful, such as a rainbow around his throne (Revelation 4 v 3). Our desire for physical beauty is evidence that we were created to be like him. But the pursuit of physical beauty should not be all-important. The beauty of the "hidden person of the heart" is what, Peter tells us, "in God's sight is very precious". Outer beauty fades and dies, but the beauty of the heart is "imperishable". Pursuing it changes the way we see ourselves and breathes life into us in a way that no lipstick or branded jeans ever could.

What our culture so often wants us to think is that our physical bodies are separate from our inner selves. Pornography, erotica and casual sex are results of this idea: separating the physical act of sex from its relational aspects. It is supposed to be possible to experience physical sexual desire without any obligation to be emotionally, relationally, and spiritually connected.

But this is impossible. The physical body cannot be separated from the inner self. When we have sex with someone, we are tying ourselves to them emotionally. Psychologists call this "enmeshment." It is a spiritual tie too; we see this in 1 Corinthians 6 v 13-16, where Paul directly compares the union of sexual partners with the union of a Christian with the Lord Jesus.

This is one reason why the Bible clearly tells us that sex is for the context of marriage between one man and one woman. God designed sex as a powerful symbol and celebration of covenant love: the expression of the deepest commitment two people can make to each other and a representation of God's own love for his people.

Old Testament prophets spoke of Israel as God's bride, even using sexual terms to describe the intimacy he desired with his people. The Hebrew word for sexual intimacy, *yada*, means "to know, to be known, to be deeply respected." This is not just about the physical act of sex but also a deep emotional and spiritual connection. In a beautiful expression of God's desire to intimately know us, Psalm 139 v 1 uses the same word: "O LORD, you have searched me and known [*yada*] me!"

Physical knowledge is linked to emotional and spiritual knowledge because each of us is one whole person. Anything that treats the physical body as separate from the inner self will lead to lack of respect and even abuse. It leads to the portrayal of dehumanizing submission in erotica. It leads to teenage girls feeling that they can only have confidence if they can send someone a nude photo of themselves. It leads to women being used for sex and then rejected. These things are not God's plan for our bodies.

TRUE BEAUTY

The verses quoted above from 1 Peter 3 talk about modest dressing in the context of relationships. Wives should not focus on their outer adornment but should consider how their actions and attitudes will affect their husbands. They can even win over non-Christians to God's kingdom by their "respectful and pure conduct" (v 2). True beauty has to do with how we relate to others and how we display God's character to those around us. It is better to spend time in God's word grooming your heart than in front of the mirror making your face beautiful.

This is not to say that our choices about our bodies don't matter. In fact they can play a part in communicating the gospel. What we wear, for example, tells a story about how the gospel has touched us and what we are living for.

When skull-and-crossbones symbols became a mainstream rage in America and many girls were embracing a dark goth style, I posed these kinds of questions to my daughters: "What story does that look tell? Is it consistent with the life-giving salvation story of your life?" I didn't make rules about what my girls could or could not wear but tried to help them to think through how their clothing choices were reflecting or not reflecting the way God had made them and the things he had done for them. Would symbols of death and darkness be a good indicator of the joy they had found in Christ? My girls don't always dress according to the rules some Christian legalists would have them obey—one wears a nose ring and the other recently dyed her hair green—and they may have ideas that are different to mine about what modest dressing looks like, but what makes me proud is that their choices for their physical bodies reflect hearts that wear the character and disposition of our God. Nothing is more beautiful than that.

Likewise, we should see sex as a portrait of God's sacred love, and not allow Satan to twist and tarnish it. We must teach respect for the body God has given each one of us.

Every woman who shares a #MeToo story has more to tell than her tweet revealed. There are too many stories of women deeply wounded by men and ultimately by our culture's acceptance of the lie that the physical body can be separated from the spiritual and emotional self. Maybe that is your story—and if it is, I am deeply sorry. If you have not done so already, please reach out to a wise Christian whom you can trust, and begin to get help and find healing. For all of us, there is a great deal of work to do as we comfort and pray with survivors in what may seem an extremely threatening world.

NO MORE SHAME

In the Garden of Eden, Adam and Eve became acutely aware of their nakedness as soon as they sinned. Their lost innocence and marred intimacy filled them with shame. In their nakedness, God provided a covering. The very first way in which God comforted his sinful people was by relieving them of shame and providing for their physical bodies.

As pastor and scholar Robert Covolo writes, "The gift of clothing reveals a God who meets us in our shameful, sinful condition and covers us through a sacrificial death."[5] Today, too, God calls us out of shame and hurt, and gives us a higher standard for our bodies, whatever we have done and whatever has been done to us. Our bodies are "members of Christ" himself, united with the Lord Jesus (1 Corinthians 6 v 15).

> *Do you not know that your body is a temple of the Holy Spirit within you, whom you have from God? You are not your own, for you were bought with a price. So glorify God in your body.*
>
> *(1 Corinthians 6 v 19-20)*

4. HOW TO WORK FOR
GOD'S GLORY

CHELSEA PATTERSON SOBOLIK

My husband and I were barely two months into our marriage and were still settling into our new life together when my professional life suddenly came crashing down around me. I was working on Capitol Hill at the time, and my boss resigned from Congress in the middle of his term. Along with the rest of his staff, I lost my job. In one day, my entire professional world shattered before my eyes, and I spent months picking up the pieces.

By God's kindness, I was able to quickly find a new job to help pay the bills; but I didn't enjoy the work. My days were spent shuffling paper, and the posture of my heart was more inclined toward grumbling than gratitude for the Lord's provision. Until that point in my life, I'd always tried to work with excellence, but I hadn't spent much time examining the topic of work in light of Scripture. But now, as I mourned the loss of my job, I also began to wrestle with what God says about work.

Work was part of God's original design, and we're all called to this good endeavor. But our work may take very different forms. Some of us are working in a traditional 9-5 office job; others are in the home, raising children; others have taken on a caregiving role for aging parents. Many of us are seeking to balance a combination of different sorts of work.

We've all faced frustrations in work, whether that's because of the tasks we are doing or the people we work alongside. But we've also likely felt deep satisfaction in our work as we've poured our hearts into it and seen fruit from those efforts.

We are easily tempted to have a misplaced view of work—whether overemphasizing it or underemphasizing it. It is vitally important to remind ourselves of the truths in Scripture, allowing God's word to inform how we think about work instead of letting other things dictate our attitude toward this huge part of all our lives.

IN THE GARDEN

In the opening verses of the Bible, we're given a front-row seat at the world's creation. The creation narrative details how God worked to design and order the world. Day after day, the Lord spoke different aspects of creation into being. The climax was the creation of humanity: the only beings made in the image of God.

> Then God said, "Let us make man in our image, after our likeness. And let them have dominion over the fish of the sea and over the birds of the heavens and over the livestock and over all the earth and over every creeping thing that creeps on the earth." So God created man in his own image, in the image of God he created him; male and female he created them. And God blessed them. And God said to them, "Be fruitful and multiply and fill the earth..."
>
> (Genesis 1 v 26-31)

After creating man and woman, the Lord rested. Everything he had done until then had been work: that means that work predated the fall. This is the case for human work too. After the Lord made Adam, Scripture tells us that "the LORD God took the man and put him in the garden of Eden to work it and keep it" (Genesis 2 v 15).

Pastor and author Tim Keller reminds us of this in his book on work, *Every Good Endeavor*:

> "*The book of Genesis leaves us with a striking truth—work was part of paradise. Work is as much a basic human need as food, beauty, rest, friendship, prayer, and sexuality; it is not simply medicine but food for our soul.*" (*page 36*)

But, if God created work for our good, why do we so often face frustrations in it?

In Genesis 3 we read about Adam and Eve's disobedience to God's commandment and how sin entered the world. This event—the fall—affected everything, including our work. For Adam, work would now be difficult and painful (Genesis 3 v 17-19). We, too, are well aware of the impact of the fall on work, as we struggle with difficult coworkers, discouragement in parenting, jealousy over others' success, or the daily effort to focus and put work in its proper place.

On this earth, Christians are called to grow in godliness and fight against sin and temptation. 2 Peter 1 v 3 tells us that "[God's] divine power has granted to us all things that pertain to life and godliness." The good news for Christians is that we aren't alone as we walk through struggle and temptation. God has given us the Holy Spirit, who lives inside us and helps us fight sin. We can also look forward to the day when all things will be made right and all wrongs righted, and we will live in a perfect world without strife or sorrow. Jesus has promised to prepare a place for us and will return to bring us to himself.

Strengthened by that knowledge, it is time to pull back the curtain and look honestly at some of the temptations we face in work.

1. OVERWORKING AND PEOPLE-PLEASING

We live in a society where busyness is glorified. Everyone wants to appear important; so we cram our calendars with appointments, meetings, and commitments—far too many of them—to make ourselves feel that our days have purpose and value.

This glorification of busyness is related to the fact that our culture is one that's seemingly always connected. Technology is a wonderful gift: with the touch of a button, you can call a friend, order groceries, share a picture of your new puppy, and so much more. But being constantly connected means that we can find ourselves tempted to always be working. Or at the very least, we can feel that we should be checking our notifications to make sure we didn't miss anything.

I love working, and I'm often fighting to establish healthy boundaries. My mind is constantly telling me that I should be working quicker, harder, and longer. Those feelings are exaggerated when I hop on social media and I'm met with posts telling me how hard others are working and what they've accomplished. The message I internalize is that to measure up to others, I must not cease to work. So I redouble my efforts to be productive and prove myself and my worth.

How might this tendency toward overworking, comparison, and people-pleasing show up in your own life? Maybe you recognize some of the following statements:

- You check in on email, when you should be checking in on the hearts of your kids.
- You "like" a few photos on Instagram, when you should be giving verbal encouragements to your friends in real life.

- You don't establish boundaries with your phone and have it readily accessible at all hours of the day and night.
- You use your phone in bed, leading to disruptive sleep patterns.

This type of behavior is exhausting and demoralizing. But it is so common.

2. PERFECTIONISM

Often coupled with overworking is a tendency toward perfectionism: a refusal to accept any standard short of perfection. Perfectionism can be a sin because we're placing ourselves, our efforts, and our striving at the center of the work, instead of seeking ultimately to please the Lord. When you have a misplaced view of work, you usurp the throne and place yourself there, thinking that your striving and strength are going to be what propel you into victory. You think that if you can just do a little more, you will be doing enough. When you fail to reach your own high standards, you feel crushed.

It's vital to remember that success doesn't ultimately lie in our hands. It belongs to the Lord. We're called to work hard and with excellence, but we're also called to simply trust the Lord with the outcome of our work. We can never be perfect. Only he is.

3. LAZINESS

When we think of laziness, we often picture someone lounging around on the sofa, binging on Netflix, and not engaging faithfully at work. But it can include behavior we might not immediately label as laziness. One of the biggest ways I've seen it play out in my own life is that I rest when I should be working, and work when I should be resting.

When I'm at work, I'll often open my computer, check email, check Twitter, check Facebook, check Slack, and then start tackling my tasks. 15 minutes later, I'll go through the entire process of checking everything again. If I'm not careful, my entire day will look like this, and I never fully and deeply engage in my work. Far too many of us approach our work this way.

I often approach rest in a similar fashion. In the evenings or on my Sabbath, when I'm supposed to be resting, I'll spend hours on social media or responding to emails that can wait. As a result, I never fully rest, and when I re-engage with work, I'm not as physically, emotionally, or spiritually rested as I could have been. It leads to a life that's never completely engaged in either work or rest—two things God tells us to do.

At its core, laziness is a mishandling of time. If we are indeed called to be stewards, we must give proper thought to how we spend our time. May we echo the prayer of the psalmist in Psalm 90 v 12:

> *Teach us to number our days*
> *that we may get a heart of wisdom.*

THE ROOT OF OUR STRUGGLES

In the cool of the Garden of Eden, Satan whispered into Eve's ear that she could be like God. That is what is at the root of many of our struggles: a self-focus instead of a God-focus. Humans are made in God's image, but we were never meant to be God. When we focus on ourselves, we often look to work to give us what only God can give—meaning, significance, acceptance, and purpose. Work is a good gift but a terrible god.

There are many other temptations we'll bump up against in our work, and that's where the local body of Christ comes into play. None of us should live or work in isolation. The Lord has called Christians to be a part of a local body of believers. I urge you to take your particular questions and frustrations to your pastor and church community. Invite them into your life and allow yourself to be deeply known and loved by the church.

FOR THE GLORY OF GOD

There's good news for us as we face and fight temptations on this side of eternity. The cross of Christ changes everything, including how we approach our work. We can rest in the finished work of Christ because we no longer have to strive for acceptance or purpose. All of that is found in Jesus. The cross frees us to work out of a new identity as beloved children of the King.

All of us have God-given passions and gifts, and we should steward those for the glory of God and the good of others. After all, Jesus has given our lives two grand purposes: to love God and to love our neighbor (Matthew 22 v 34-40).

I have a sticky note on my computer with Colossians 3 v 23 (NIV) written on it:

> *Whatever you do, work at it with all your heart, as working for the Lord, not for human masters.*

As I'm engaging in my daily work, I'm reminded that my work is ultimately for King Jesus. When we remember that we're called to serve him, our joys and sorrows will be less tied to victories and successes in our work and instead will be securely tethered to our identity in Christ.

What does it mean to actually work for the glory of God? One of the most important things to remember is that we are not our own, and our actions don't merely reflect upon ourselves. They reflect on God. "We are ambassadors for Christ, God making his appeal through us" (2 Corinthians 5 v 20). Working for God's glory means that we should be intentional in seeking to love the Lord with all of our mind, heart and soul, and to love our neighbor as ourselves. We can structure our time with this in mind.

Everything we do matters to God, and we can use our words and deeds to point others to the Lord. That means we can glorify God in many different seasons and circumstances. So...

If you're changing a child's diaper, do it for God's glory.

If you're writing an email, do it for God's glory.

If you're greeting a customer, do it for God's glory.

If you're cooking dinner for your family, do it for God's glory.

A quote often attributed to the great Reformer Martin Luther makes this point:

> *"The maid who sweeps her kitchen is doing the will of God just as much as the monk who prays—not because she may sing a Christian hymn as she sweeps, but because God loves clean floors. The Christian shoemaker does his Christian duty not by putting little crosses on the shoes, but by making good shoes, because God is interested in good craftsmanship."*

All work is valuable to the Lord, and all work matters. So, if you're stuck at a job you don't enjoy, or you lose your job suddenly as I did, remember that that time isn't wasted. The Lord can use it, and has used it, to help you love him and love your neighbor better.

After I graduated from college, I began an application process with a missions agency. I'd spent years planning to move overseas and devote myself to ministry. But as I was in the midst of the process, I sensed the Lord asking me to stop. I obeyed his voice, even though I was confused. Later I realized how much pride was in my heart. I'd bought into the lie that being a missionary was more godly than anything else, and subconsciously I believed that the Lord would love me more if I devoted myself to full-time ministry. I thought that full-time ministry counted in God's economy more than regular work.

This view was narrow, limited, and, frankly, unbiblical. The Lord sovereignly places us in different spheres of influence and work, and we all have the opportunity to shine the light of Christ wherever we go—even if our job title doesn't include "ministry."

In everything we do, there's a deeper and truer reality than what we can see. What we do on earth matters because it shapes us and the people around us. When we seek to love God and others in what we do, we're practicing for heaven. We're training and rehearsing for eternity, which will be filled with the glory of God.

STOPPING WORK

Working for God's glory means that we can rest from work without feeling guilty.

Rest reminds us that God is God and we are not. We weren't created to be limitless. We were created to be dependent creatures, in need of our regular rest and sleep.

The first two verses of Psalm 127 remind us of the Lord's sovereignty and our responsibility to trust and rest in him:

> *Unless the LORD builds the house,*
> *those who build it labor in vain.*
> *Unless the LORD watches over the city,*
> *the watchman stays awake in vain.*
> *It is in vain that you rise up early*
> *and go late to rest,*
> *eating the bread of anxious toil;*
> *for he gives to his beloved sleep.*

Observing the Sabbath is a commandment that the Lord gives to his people for their good, yet many Western Christians approach it as a suggestion. While we don't have to be legalistic about observing a Sabbath—using it to condemn people who don't rest, as the Pharisees did—we shouldn't ignore it. God created us to work six days and rest one day. As with work, a Sabbath rest is good for us. We ought to reorient our time to honor the Lord, observing the rhythms in which he ordered the world.

Psalm 127 shows us that it's foolish to pretend that we're above the commandments of the Lord. Consider what a regular Sabbath looks like for you and your family. Different seasons of life will affect what rest looks like, but I urge you to give regular rhythms of Sabbath serious prayer and consideration.

Besides going to church and spending time with my church family, I like to fill my Sabbaths with some of my favorite life-giving activities—going for a walk outside, journaling, baking, napping, and reading good books. Another practice that's extremely beneficial is building in time to step away from your phone and social media. Try setting daily boundaries on technology use. Our phones can easily become our masters if we're not careful, and setting boundaries helps with putting them in their proper place.

When you stop work, put down your phone, and rest, you are refusing to be ruled by a desire to please people; you are resisting the perfectionist impulse to do just a little more; and you are recharging yourself with the energy you need to avoid falling into laziness. You are embracing a biblical view of work: one that values work highly and takes it seriously, yet that acknowledges that it is loving the Lord that matters most of all.

As you finish this chapter I'd like to encourage you to pause and pray. Ask the Lord to give you wisdom on navigating the work season you find yourself in. Ask him to teach you what it means to love God and love your neighbor through your work. Ask him to reveal any idols you might be clinging onto instead of surrendering all of your life to him.

I hope you may find deep and rich fulfillment in your work. But whether you do or you don't, most of all I hope you may rest in Jesus' promise that he's coming to make all things new. Together let's look forward to the day when we'll work without struggle and rest with the deepest imaginable joy.

5. THE VALUE OF
LITERATURE

KAREN SWALLOW PRIOR

Parents are often told to read to their children. It helps children to learn to read for themselves if we read to them—regularly and often—from a very young age. Nearly all little children love stories and rhymes, and can be encouraged to take pleasure and delight in language and books. Parents should cultivate that early love for as long as they can.

As we grow up, we all continue to read in some way. We read textbooks while in school in order to learn. We read newspapers and magazines in order to be informed. As Christians, we read the Bible in order to know God and grow in him. But for too many, something happens to strip away the natural love of reading stories. We don't read books for pleasure in the way that children do. We may make sure we have time for books on theology and Christian living, but we don't bother venturing into other genres.

But the theologian Kevin Vanhoozer says that imagination, trained and developed by reading literature, is "a vital ingredient" in the believer's sanctification.[1] We shouldn't think of books as merely an educational tool (though they are a very effective one). Reading stories and loving language can help us to pursue God and love his people more.

THE POWER OF THE WORD

In the beginning was the Word, and the Word was with God, and the Word was God. He was with God in the beginning. Through him all things were made; without him nothing was made that has been made.

(John 1 v 1-3)

The Bible uses "word" (or *logos* in the original Greek) to refer directly both to Christ and to Scripture, the revealed word of God. This is not a coincidence! Christianity is a religion of the word. God reveals himself through words—supremely through the words of Scripture. The word *logos* is the one from which we get our word "logical." It has to do with rationality and order.

This describes the way words work, whether written or spoken. Unlike visual messages or images, words must be understood in a linear, logical fashion. Imagine taking all the words from a favorite passage in a book and scattering them across a piece of paper. The very words that carried so much meaning in their linear order would now make no sense whatsoever. It is in the nature of words—and of all literature—to present the meaning they contain in a logical, linear way.

This reveals something of the nature of God, too, as well as the way he works through time toward redemption. God is a God of order, rationality, and reason. This is why he reveals himself to us in the word. Christ is called the Word partly because he represents the order of the universe; it was through him that the ordered creation was made. The very form that literature takes reflects this aspect of God's nature.

But it is not just on this conceptual level that Christianity is a religion of the word. Christ's life, the teaching of the apostles, and the history of the spread of Christianity are all preserved in written form: the Gospels (a word which literally means "good story"), the book of Acts, and the letters. The early church knew that it was vital to compile the New Testament from these texts which are the inspired word of God. The first centuries of the church were marked by additional writings which, although subordinate to the Scriptures, also sustained and taught new believers—and can continue to teach us today.

Later, the Protestant Reformation renewed this emphasis on the written word. In fact, the defining moment of the movement involved a written text—Luther's 95 Theses—being nailed on a door for all to see. Key to the Reformation was the idea that people should be able to read God's word in their own language. Literacy was central to the entire Reformation and the church and culture it created.

Some of the world's great literature has been produced by writers and thinkers who were Christians (at least in respect of their worldview): John Milton's *Paradise Lost*; John Bunyan's *The Pilgrim's Progress*; Daniel Defoe's *Robinson Crusoe*; Jonathan Swift's *Gulliver's Travels*; Jane Austen's *Pride and Prejudice*; Charlotte Brontë's *Jane Eyre*. The list goes on. But in contemporary times, you might observe that less great literature comes from Christian writers. This is a reason for Christians to read (and write!) more literature. The lack of strong literary writing in the church today is the result of starvation: we have a less robust understanding and appreciation of literary art than our forebears. This is a departure from the Protestant tradition. Cultivating the habit of reading in the church can help us to reclaim our own heritage.

ACTS OF IMAGINATION

Of course, reading literature is not just for those who have aspirations to write literature of their own. It is something that is open to all of us to do, whether or not we are already used to reading.

There are some who enjoy books on theology and Christian living but stay away from novels and poetry. It's true that it is well worth reading books specifically designed to help us grow as Christians. But just as an athlete training for a marathon must vary her exercise and train in a variety of ways to maximize her performance in the race, so a reader will find that reading various types of books can strengthen her vocabulary, comprehension, and critical thinking skills. These things can enhance our enjoyment and understanding of the Bible and theology books.

For example, some of the best works of theology use poetic language and figures of speech to present powerful truths even more powerfully. The mind exercised by reading poetry or poetic prose is often more receptive to the tendrils of truth contained in such literary language. This goes for Scripture, too. The Bible is composed of various literary genres—each with its own rules and demands—and the language of the Bible is some of the most beautiful and most-cited in the world. Improving our reading skills helps us to understand and appreciate God's revealed word as he speaks to us through it by his Spirit.

Literature also trains and forms our minds more generally. We are by nature creatures of imagination, and the way we form and feed the imagination is no small matter. We need imaginations which seek God and connect our story to his: which look out for ways in which he is working in our lives and the lives of those around us.

God expressed delight in his created world by declaring that it was good, and he wants his image bearers, too, to experience delight in what is good. One way we can appreciate the world around us is through books. The better we become at reading, and the more thoroughly and carefully we read, the more we will enjoy both language and the God-created world that language describes.

Reading good literature allows us to delight in a story well told, a phrase well turned, a description well captured, or a truth well expressed. That is good stewardship of God's wonderful gift of language. And becoming aware of these things in books will help us to take notice of what we see in the world around us and to find meaning in it. Instead of walking straight past the fuzzy pink slipper left on the sidewalk, we might wonder how it got there and where its partner is. Instead of focusing on our work or the music in our headphones on the train, we might look at the people around us and wonder where they are going and what experiences have brought them this far. These are small, everyday examples of the use of human imagination. But they are different only in degree from the big, universal questions about the human condition: Who am I? Where did I come from? What is the meaning of my life?

The answers to these questions are found only in the word of God. But it is in little acts of imagination that such questioning can begin.

WHATEVER IS TRUE...

Life may be long, but the list of books that exist in the world is even longer. A lifetime of reading will never come close to getting through even a fraction of the good books that are out there. It can seem overwhelming to the would-be reader who doesn't know where to start.

One verse in Paul's letter to the Philippians is often cited as a good principle for choosing what to read.

> *Finally, brothers, whatever is true, whatever is honorable, whatever is just, whatever is pure, whatever is lovely, whatever is commendable, if there is any excellence, if there is anything worthy of praise, think about these things.* (Philippians 4 v 8)

When we apply this verse to our reading habits, it may seem at first glance that we should read only literature that is happy and light—that is not too dark and despairing, and that doesn't contain sin. But a deeper understanding of Paul's meaning will help us to see how to practice discernment not only in our choice of reading material but also in the way we read.

Consider the word "pure," for example. Another word for "purity" is "integrity." A work that has integrity is one that doesn't lie about the human experience or cheat its way to a happy ending. It might present a character that is deeply flawed but also likeable—just like a real person. The reader will be required to do some hard, honest work of examination, both of the book and of themselves. We must try to understand the complexity of such a character and notice our own responses to him or her.

The word "true" makes this even clearer. Some of the most innocent and cheerful works of literature are the ones that are the least true. Some books may present us with truth that hurts: depictions of suffering and pain, or stories about sin which we recognize in ourselves. Such things may be difficult to read, but that does not necessarily mean that it is bad for us to do so.

This verse also talks about what is "commendable" and "worthy of praise." When applied to books, these phrases call readers to consider a work's reputation among those who know literature well. Works that have passed the test of time and have received universal acclaim can usually be considered excellent and praiseworthy. Of course, some of these texts can be difficult because of old-fashioned language or a setting that demands historical knowledge. We should be realistic about our own reading skills and experience. But we shouldn't be afraid of classic literature just because it may be challenging. If it is excellent and praiseworthy, it is worth reading.

The Bible also tells us that not all things that are lawful are necessarily helpful (1 Corinthians 10 v 23). Some books may be unhelpful for particular people to read, perhaps because they tempt them to indulge in a particular sin. Likewise, a trained literary scholar may derive great benefit from a book which would not serve a less experienced reader in the same way. We need to ask the Holy Spirit to help us as we think critically about our reading choices, seeking to understand how a work may affect us. As we strive toward maturity in our thinking and in our ability to face what the world is like, we need to learn to distinguish between a healthy challenge and a stumbling block.

A GREAT GIFT

Reading is a wonderful way of helping children to learn. It's not just that it teaches them language and helps them develop their own reading and writing skills. It also introduces them to people, places, and experiences that they may not face directly. It is the same for any of us: reading expands our mental, emotional, and imaginative horizons. As Christians seeking to love those around us, we can read in order to develop empathy and compassion for our real-life neighbors.

But reading also leads us to delight in the world our God has created: the endless variety of people, places and creatures he has made. There is so much to enjoy in his gifts to us of imagination, creativity, and language. This is the best reason of all to read to children and to teach them using books. I encourage people of any age to read not only the things they feel they "should" read, but also the things they like to read. Science fiction, historical novels, romance, crime, nature writing, poetry, plays, non-fiction. Let reading be delightful! And pray that reading may lead you closer to the Lord.

If you read very little or not at all, try devoting just half an hour today to it—perhaps before bed. Or download audiobooks and listen while you exercise or drive.

For further help and ideas, let me recommend a few books about books that serve as guides to increasing one's reading fare:

- *How to Read a Book* by Mortimer Adler and Charles Van Doren
- *Invitation to the Classics: A Guide to Books You've Always Wanted to Read* by Os Guinness
- *The Pleasures of Reading in an Age of Distraction* by Alan Jacobs
- *Booked: Literature in the Soul of Me* by Karen Swallow Prior
- *On Reading Well: Finding the Good Life Through Great Books* by Karen Swallow Prior
- *Lit: A Christian Guide to Reading Books* by Tony Reinke
- *The Christian Imagination: The Practice of Faith in Literature and Writing* by Leland Ryken
- *Reading for the Common Good: How Books Help Our Churches and Neighborhoods Flourish* by C. Christopher Smith
- *Reading Between the Lines* by Gene Edward Veith

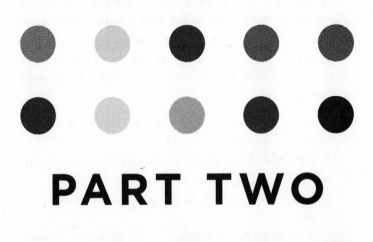

PART TWO

LISTENING WELL

LISTENING WELL:

INTRODUCTION TO PART 2

TRILLIA NEWBELL AND
JACKIE HILL PERRY

Jesus commanded his disciples to "go and make disciples of all nations" (Matthew 28 v 19), but most of us feel pretty unsure about how to do that. Maybe we admire foreign missionaries or local church ministers and wish that our contribution to God's kingdom could be as great as theirs. Maybe our lives get filled with day-to-day concerns, and we forget about the Great Commission altogether.

So how can we—as ordinary women living ordinary lives, where the call to missions isn't associated with our daily work—be faithful to Jesus' command? And how can we be contented with our service in the kingdom of God?

The truth is that as soon as you engage with someone who isn't you, you hit on an opportunity to make disciples of all nations. As soon as you start asking questions about the messages and narratives you hear in the world around you, you are engaging with different cultures and with worldviews that are not your own. Practicing cultural engagement is a means to win people for Christ.

For four years I (Jackie) had a job training volunteers to work with inner city youth in Chicago. These kids mostly didn't know their dads and were living in an environment where people were dying around them all the time, while probably 90% of our volunteers were white women with good jobs and stable families. I had to help these women manage the cultural conflict.

The mentors were seeking to bring these kids to faith, but that didn't mean assimilating them to their own culture. They had to try to understand where the cultural differences were in order to avoid simply condemning the inner-city culture. They also had to make sure they were actually teaching the kids truth when it came to the gospel. Often their own story of faith looked very different from the journey the kids were on, and so they couldn't rely on their own experience; they needed to have a solid, biblical understanding of what salvation actually is.

In every context, the truth remains the same. I (Trillia) have spent time in inner-city youth ministry caring for children who were seeing murder and drug use. Obviously murder and drug use aren't present in every inner-city context, but in this particular ministry, these children needed a listening ear and the persistent presence of a mentor—and the gospel and love of Jesus clearly spoken over them. And over the past few years I have taught the Bible in a women's rehab center. In each of these contexts, my own life and culture were different to those of the people I was working with, but the truth remained the same, and the need for that truth was evident for their hearts as well as my own. The gospel has power.

The Great Commission requires us to step outside of what is comfortable for us and engage with people from different backgrounds. If part of being a disciple is seeking to disciple others, then breaking out of your own cultural world and stepping into someone else's is necessary, even if it is hard.

That doesn't mean that everyone will find themselves in situations where sharing the gospel is hard. Our ordinary means may involve talking to the clerk at the grocery store or engaging with our next-door neighbor. Either way, your faith is sharpened as you become more aware of the things and circumstances that influence you, and you learn to let the Bible shape your thinking instead. And as you build relationships with individuals who otherwise live a world away from Christian influences, you will give them the chance to hear and respond to the gospel, which is good news for all people.

This mission might mean re-examining our attitudes toward immigrants and minority populations. It might mean rethinking the way we listen to the news or other ways in which we participate in national conversations about issues like race and inequality. It might also simply be a matter of being hospitable: inviting people over, having dinner, asking questions, listening.

How beautiful it is when you and I live in the world beyond just our families: when we open our doors and engage with the wider world around us. When we do this, we need to remind ourselves that we're not going to save people out of their culture; instead we should try to understand where they come from and how the gospel speaks into that.

The chapters in this section start to explore how we can listen better, being thoughtful not just about our own cultural influences, assumptions, and likes but also about the cultures of others. This section shows the importance of loving our neighbors and suggests some ways of actually doing that—from the simple act of trying new foods to the possibility of engaging in national debates.

Of course, first we have to be willing. Loving our neighbors may make us uncomfortable, and we need to ask God for humility. Remember that even though you may want to stay in your yard, that isn't what God has called you to do. With his help, go ahead. Go on across the street, get past the dogs, and knock on the door. They probably don't have cookies, but they might have some chitlins, and that's alright.

6. INVITING OTHERS
TO OUR HOMES

COURTNEY REISSIG

I love to cook. I love to experiment with recipes. But while I do enjoy trying new things, I am not adventurous when it comes to ingredients I don't understand. If I don't know what something is for, I won't buy it. If I can't pronounce a recipe's name, I won't make it. If it is something I've never heard of, I will pass over it. As a result, my family continues to eat the same types of food and never strays from what is familiar to us. We miss out on a world of food combinations and ingredients that are probably really good because I don't take the time to branch out a little more.

I think that's often what we do with people who are different from us. People of different ethnicities, for example. People from other cultures. People who speak other languages or uphold other traditions. People who have different personalities than our own. It can seem like hard work to branch out and cultivate such relationships.

We don't need a large-scale sociological experiment to tell us that we tend to gravitate toward people who are like us. This becomes a problem when our preferences and our choices move away from things like food and ingredients to people and ethnicities. Missing out on a new meal would be disappointing; but missing out on relationships with fellow image-bearers is far more serious. Thankfully, the Bible is not silent on such things. Throughout Scripture, we see God calling his people to hospitality. The Israelites were commanded to welcome strangers—people not like them (Leviticus 19 v 34; Deuteronomy 10 v 19). This call to welcoming diversity in our homes and lives carried over into the new covenant: the New Testament writers repeatedly speak to the necessity of hospitality—even to the point of listing it as a qualification for an elder (1 Timothy 3 v 2).

When we speak of hospitality, it often conjures up images of fancy dinner parties or entertaining. But that is not the way the Bible speaks of hospitality—nor the way I am going to speak of it in this chapter.

Hospitality, as I see it, is about living a life of welcome. That can include many contexts and many actions—it doesn't have to involve food, for example. But in this chapter, I will specifically talk about a life of welcome that invites others into our homes. This may sometimes be at the expense of what is comfortable for us, especially when we invite people who come from different backgrounds than our own; but it is a way of reflecting the diversity of God's creation and heeding his call for all people to unite around his throne. Our homes can be the vehicle by which we display God's hospitality— inviting them not just to the dinner table but into the family of God.

There is one passage that speaks especially clearly about the call to hospitality even when our guests might be different than us. It will help us get our bearings as we talk about using our homes for the purpose of hospitality.

Let brotherly love continue. Do not neglect to show hospitality to strangers, for thereby some have entertained angels unawares. Remember those who are in prison,

as though in prison with them, and those who are
mistreated, since you also are in the body.
(Hebrews 13 v 1-3)

At first glance, you might not see it, but a closer look helps us see that the writer of Hebrews is calling Christians outside of themselves. In the context of the book, persecution was all around. So here at the end of the book, he reminds the church again to be hospitable to strangers—people who might not be like them—and those in prison.

Elsewhere, the writer of Hebrews reminds them of their great sacrifice for those who were in prison (Hebrews 10 v 34). So this was not a new command but one which they were already obeying. The normative practice for these Christians was to practice hospitality, to care for those in prison, and to live like something better awaited them. They were all united under the lordship of Christ, from the poor and oppressed to the rich and influential. They might have had different circumstances, but the promise they all possessed—the hope of Christ and his city that is to come—could never be taken from them. So they were able to serve freely even those who could so readily have been forgotten as they languished in prison.

It is easy to forget such people. That's true when life is going well, because we get settled into comfortable patterns and stop remembering to reach out. But it can be even harder to remember this command when life is difficult or when you are yourself facing persecution, as the first readers of the book of Hebrews were. That is why the writer warns them, "Do not neglect" but "remember."

WELCOMING STRANGERS

We, too, need to tell one another, "'Do not neglect' but 'remember' to show hospitality to strangers."

That includes anyone who is different than us—people of other ethnicities, other countries, or other economic backgrounds; and people we find difficult or simply seem to have nothing in common with.

For some of us this may seem like too great a task. Maybe everyone you know is from the same background as you, and you don't know how to find friends who come from different communities. Maybe you have had bad experiences in the past and are afraid to engage in conversations and interactions that could be painful. Maybe you are overwhelmed by the bias and prejudice you see around you and wonder what difference your contribution could make. Maybe you simply feel that you have enough to worry about already.

This is where the command in Hebrews is so helpful to us. "Remember to show hospitality to strangers," the writer says. Why do we need to remember? Because it is hard! It is comfortable to be around the familiar. It is uncomfortable to make the effort to get to know strangers. But we must take seriously the call to remember to serve and welcome such people.

First, this means welcoming other Christians, however different they may be. Our brothers and sisters might look, sound, act, or think differently than we do, but we all have the same origin, and in the body of Christ we all have the same inheritance (Galatians 3 v 28). When one of us is suffering, we all ultimately suffer. When one of us is mistreated, the image of God is being maligned. We are all part of the same body—the body of Christ.

Second, it also means welcoming non-Christians, however different they may be. Remember, God is a welcoming God: he is calling a people to himself from every tribe, tongue, and nation. Often one of the first steps people make toward God is through the welcome of those who call him Father. When we invite non-Christians into our homes, we are their point of contact with the Savior. As we pray over our food before the meal, we show that we have a God who is the giver of all good things (James 1 v 17). As we give of our time so they can come into our home, we show that we have a better hope in heaven than simply leisure, pleasure, and comfort here on earth. Being invited into the home of another is startling to an unbeliever sometimes, but it also can be God's means of grace in his or her life.

It is helpful to remember that we were all once strangers, both spiritually and socially. Our comfort in this life is owing to the welcoming hospitality of someone else.

Maybe you were new to a school, and someone introduced herself to you. You were the stranger, and she made a way for you. Maybe you were new to a church or neighborhood, and your neighbors or church members kept pursuing you. You were the stranger, and they made a way for you. But the greatest example of all is seen in the God of the universe welcoming us—welcoming you—into his family. You brought nothing to the table, yet God welcomed you and gave you a place in his kingdom. You were a stranger, and he made a way for you.

We are here by the hospitality of another. This is why we welcome the stranger: to continue that legacy.

HOW TO BEGIN

So how should you start? You see the welcome of God in your own life and embrace his command to welcome strangers. What's your next step?

Sometimes it is hard to see how you can be used in God's plan of saving people from all nations. Maybe you have an overwhelming job and little time for extra activities. Or maybe you have small children and cannot see how you can add any more people into your life. I get it. I have been in the same situation (and still am in a lot of ways). The rest of the chapter is going to include simple practical ways you can use your home to be a place of welcome. You could even pick one thing for the entire year. Start small. Or start big. The point is to see your home as a place where hospitality can happen, even if you are limited in time or resources.

First, pray for a humble, soft heart toward those you don't find it easy to make connections with. We should all ask God to reveal where we have been prejudiced or selfish in the past, and ask him to make us sensitive and empathetic in the future. Thankfully, God delights to answer broken-hearted, humble prayers (Psalm 51 v 17). Starting here is a way of acknowledging that only he can do the work of reconciliation. It's an opportunity for dependence on the God who created us all in his image.

The next step is to listen well. Listen to others and try to understand their perspective. That might mean reading books, listening to podcasts, watching documentaries, talking to friends, or getting to know new neighbors. It's easy to form a quick opinion about particular groups or individuals as an outsider looking in, but Christians are to be slow to speak and to judge (James 1 v 19; Matthew 7 v 1-2). Reading first-hand accounts of different cultures or experiences and talking to flesh-and-blood people are things that will help us truly understand others.

In listening and understanding where others might come from, we remove the barriers that keep us from inviting them into our homes in the first place. We don't welcome strangers who seem different and maybe even scary. But if we get to know them as God's image-bearers, who in many ways are just like us, it makes welcoming them much easier.

We should not be naive: there will be some whom it would be unwise to invite straight into our homes, either because they have difficult needs which we cannot meet, or even because they have malicious intentions. It is best to consult your church leaders about how to have a welcoming disposition toward such people without putting yourself or your family at risk. This is why prayer and careful listening are good first steps in hospitality.

I wanted to provide some examples of this kind of openness which come from people who live in places and situations that are different than mine. So here are two other contributors to this book, sharing their own ideas about how we can prepare ourselves and our homes to welcome strangers more easily.

First, the film critic Alissa Wilkinson:

"We have access nowadays to movies from all over the world. Netflix has many wonderful, wonderful films that can give you a window into different cultures and the different ways people around the world think.

Sometimes people say to me, 'I don't want to watch that because it's subtitled.' But reading isn't something you don't know how to do! If anything, watching subtitled films is easier because you don't have to worry about hearing every little word that is said.

It's worth getting used to subtitles because some of the best and most interesting work in film is being done in places all around the world. Not only are these films high-quality art, but they are also valuable as cultural education. You can learn a lot about other religions— watching films from Iran and Iraq will teach you a great deal about Islam, for example. And there they are, right there in your living room already.

You don't even have to try to have a conversation with these filmmakers; you just get to sit there and experience their world as they portray it. That's a low-stakes way to start to understand the world better."

Second, Trillia Newbell, author, editor of this book, and my dear friend:

"One summer I had my kids choose a list of countries they wanted to learn about. Each week we had a different country. We would read about its history; we would listen to its music, and watch music videos and dance around to them; and I would make a dish from that country for everyone to try. It wasn't 'Christian'—I was just teaching them about another culture. It was really fun.

And it got my neighbors involved. A friend of mine is married to a Romanian, and she heard what I was doing and cooked a dish for the kids. They got to hear the Romanian language and engage in that specific culture, and my friend got to participate in our family and see how our home life works.

Anyone can do this, whether you have kids or not; hanging out and cooking together with a friend is a powerful thing. It's living life together, getting to know your neighbors, and engaging in the lives of others. It's a way of reaching out and inviting people in. Sometimes we think we have to do something glamorous or impressive, or that we have to give people a complete gospel outline in every conversation in order for it to really count as serving the Lord. But if you are devoutly trying to get to know your neighbor and contribute to your community and be faithful to your church, that counts."

LOOKING AROUND YOU

I've spoken about prayer and about how we can develop an attitude of listening to and welcoming other perspectives. These things naturally lead us into actually welcoming strangers into our own homes.

God has given each one of us a context in which to live; he has placed us here not for ourselves but for others. Serving him always includes reaching out. You don't even necessarily need to go anywhere. You simply need eyes to look around at the place where God has planted you.

You usually don't have to look far to find people who come from a different background than you. Perhaps you live in a community with a high immigrant population. Perhaps you worship or work alongside someone of a different ethnicity, or your children have friends who come from a different socio-economic background.

As we've seen, welcoming others who are different from ourselves can start with things as simple as trying out new foods. We just need to begin to see our own homes and familiar places for what they are: opportunities. Maybe you are like me, and the thought of trying out a new ingredient scares you. That is a good place to start. You might be surprised by the new food. Then maybe that newfound bravery moves into inviting a boy from your son's class for dinner.

My husband and I have found that one of the easiest ways to welcome "strangers" into our own home is through our kids' school. When our twins started there, we wanted to be intentional about engaging with other people in the public school system. Our school has an active parental involvement, so we met a number of other parents who also wanted to get to know one another through an open-house party. We decided to host an end-of-the-year party at our home for all of the families in the boys' class. I'll be honest: at first, I was really nervous that no one would come—or at least they would think it strange that we wanted to invite twenty other families to our house for a party. But to my surprise, people were excited—even though it rained for most of it and we had to move the party to our garage.

We always knew our school was filled with families from a variety of backgrounds (ethnic, socio-economic, etc), but it was only when we had them all crowded around our folding tables in the garage that we realized that in welcoming a kindergarten class into our home, we were also inviting the nations. It was a simple party, but even in its simplicity we saw potential for hope-infused relationships as we shared our family story with others. We realized that we all aren't as different as we seem.

That is what hospitality often does. In welcoming others who might seem vastly different, we find that our shared humanity includes shared burdens and shared joys. My husband and I hope to continue the tradition of the end-of-the-year party for years to come.

There are so many ways to step out of our comfort zones, listen to the wider world, and welcome people from all nations, tribes and tongues, right from within our own homes and communities. We don't have to make big, flashy, impressive gestures. Ordinary, everyday choices will do: small things that every one of us can do to serve Christ and love his world by being hospitable in the contexts in which he has placed us.

7. LOVING THE STRANGER, LOVING THE IMMIGRANT

JENNY YANG

I pulled into the driveway of the home of Nader, Ramya, and their four children: a Syrian refugee family who had resettled to Baltimore, MD. When I opened the car door, the father, Nader, scooped up my one-year-old son. David started crying immediately. But Nader was undeterred. He hugged him warmly, bounced him up and down, and went inside to find a toy bicycle for him to play with.

The Kassab family (not their real name) come from an area in Syria called Daara, known as "the cradle of the Syrian revolution"—the place where protests sparked the beginning of the uprising of 2011. After a water tank behind their house was bombed and part of their home was damaged, Nader and his family fled from Daara into Jordan. Although Syria used to be the second-largest host country to refugees, it's now the country that produces them in the largest numbers. Three-quarters of these Syrian refugees are women and children.

Today we are witnessing the greatest number of people forcibly displaced from their homes since World War II. Conflicts which cause large refugee outflows are lasting longer than expected, as solutions seem less and less achievable. Many refugees desire to go back home eventually, but the reality is that they often stay as refugees in surrounding countries for years—even decades—on end.

A small, select number of refugees, however, are able to resettle in a third country, like the United States of America. The United States at one point used to receive the largest number of refugees of any country—which, however, represented less than 0.5 percent of the world's refugees. Since the inception of its refugee resettlement program in 1980, the US has received over 3 million refugees. Many of these have been welcomed by churches into their communities and homes.

But receiving this small number of refugees—those such as the Kassab family—has not been without controversy in the United States. Questions about national security and national identity have dominated the national debate. After the terrorist bombings in Paris in November 2015, for example, 31 state governors in the United States said they did not want Syrian refugees resettled in their state, even though refugees had not been involved in carrying out the attacks.

Refugees are part of the larger category of immigrants. An immigrant is anyone who has left his or her home to move to another country, whether voluntarily or not. Reasons could include poverty or humanitarian disaster. While conversations around migration have centered on economics and national security, there has often been a particular concern about refugees because they're fleeing conflict areas. But a refugee is someone who has left his or her country because of a well-founded fear of persecution based on race, religion, nationality, political opinion or membership in a particular social group. Refugees are the victims, not the perpetrators, of terrorism, and our policies should reflect a compassionate concern for their protection and well-being. Certainly, we need to ask the right questions to ensure that our country doesn't admit anyone who intends to do us harm; but security doesn't have to come at the expense of compassion.

For followers of Christ, there are deeper questions concerning whether and how we should welcome these refugees. And we should start with an understanding of what the Scriptures teach us about God and the movement of people.

BIBLE IMMIGRANTS

Many of the heroes and heroines of the biblical narrative were immigrants themselves. Abraham was called by God to leave his homeland to go to another land that God would show him. Leaving everything that was comfortable and familiar was a testament to his faith in God and to God's faithfulness to him. Ruth was a Moabite woman who followed her widowed mother-in-law into Israel and became a migrant worker, before she was noticed by Boaz. The whole of God's people was displaced in the exodus story; from being "strangers in the land of Egypt" (Leviticus 19 v 34), they journeyed through the desert for 40 years before reaching their new home. Starting from the earliest biblical stories, migration has been not only a fact of life but also a way for people to draw closer to God.

Immigrants are recognized in Scripture as particularly vulnerable, along with orphans and widows; these were individuals without societal or family support. In the Old Testament, God's people were repeatedly called to love and to seek justice for immigrants. "He executes justice for the fatherless and the widow, and loves the sojourner, giving him food and clothing" (Deuteronomy 10 v 18; see also Deuteronomy 10 v 17, 19; Psalm 146 v 9; Zechariah 7 v 10; and Malachi 3 v 5, among others). *Ger*, the Hebrew word closest to the English word "immigrant," appears 92 times in the Old Testament alone, as God repeatedly makes provision for such individuals.

But this idea of loving the stranger is not limited to the Old Testament. After all, the most notable refugee in Scripture was

Jesus: a Middle-Eastern refugee whose family fled to Egypt to avoid the massacre ordered by Herod.

TRUE HOSPITALITY

Jesus tells us in Matthew 25 v 40 that when we serve others, we are serving him: "As you did it to one of the least of these my brothers, you did it to me." One of his examples is this:

I was a stranger and you welcomed me. (v 35)

Jesus knew intimately from his childhood what it was like to be an unwelcomed stranger, and he urges us to show hospitality to others who experience the same thing.

Jesus is talking here about welcoming other believers; but Christians are also called to love even our enemies (Matthew 5 v 44)—like the Good Samaritan in Luke 10. This is a radical hospitality that is sacrificial and costly. It is deeper than the usual American hospitality which centers around our family and friends. The word for biblical hospitality is *philoxenia*, which literally means "love of the stranger"; it is the opposite of xenophobia. True hospitality means welcoming the stranger, the other, into our community. Scripture challenges us to show this kind of hospitality (Luke 14 v 8-11). When we get to know strangers, we may be entertaining angels without knowing it (Hebrews 13 v 2).

Not only this, but in getting to know new neighbors from parts of the world we may never visit, we find opportunities to reach the nations for Christ without ever leaving our own neighborhoods. Many refugees come from areas where they have never heard the gospel before. Sharing the good news with them is a way of fulfilling Jesus' command to "make disciples of all nations" (Matthew 28 v 19).

World Relief, the charity in which I work, recently partnered with a church in Nashville, TN, that showed the *Jesus* video to a group of traditionally Buddhist Bhutanese refugees who had resettled in their city. This movie shares the life and story of Jesus Christ through film in a simple, powerful way that can translate to many cultures. Many of them came to know Christ, and dozens were baptized in one local church service. We've also seen Iraqi and Syrian refugees come to accept the Lord as their personal Savior after having vivid dreams about Jesus.

Others arrive as vibrant believers already. They are not just recipients but agents of mission, empowered to reach others with the gospel message. Many Christians throughout Europe and the Middle East attest to how refugees are transforming the life of their church in positive ways. A group of churches in Italy, for example, created Mediterranean Hope, an organization which helps refugees with the processing of their visas and has set up cultural centers to help with refugee integration.[1] A German church has served as a shelter for Iraqi Yazidis who lived in fear of being deported back to danger.[2] A church in Brussels has also helped facilitate the integration of asylum seekers coming from Latin America; now their services have asylum seekers worshiping God alongside politicians and locals.[3] Church leaders throughout Europe also came together to issue a statement in December 2018 in which they said, "We commit to more fervently articulating and working towards our vision of an inclusive and participatory society— for newly arrived and all inhabitants."[4] The truth is that migration is not just changing the face of our own country; by bringing Christians from across the world together into the same congregations, it is changing the face of the church.

This should not surprise us. Acts 17 v 26-27 says:

And [God] made from one man every nation of mankind to live on all the face of the earth, having determined allotted periods and the boundaries of their dwelling place, that they should seek God, and perhaps feel their way toward him and find him.

Scripture challenges us to view migration not as a mere, incidental human interaction but as a divinely orchestrated plan to lead people from all nations to seek God.

LOVING THE STRANGER

The bottom line is that when I welcome refugees, I don't do it out of pity or guilt or charity. I do it simply because it's what Christ did for me. He welcomed me as an outsider into the fold of grace and declared that I am his. I owe the same hospitality to others, regardless of where they're from or how they practice their faith.

I should seek to be someone to whom Jesus could say, "I was a stranger and you welcomed me." I can invite immigrants into my home and my community. For example, I have volunteered with a local refugee-resettlement agency where I was set up with a refugee family from Iran to help in their transition to the United States. I visited with them weekly, just having conversations and helping them with any school paperwork they had to fill out. I often felt I received more than I gave as the family cooked delicious food for me and became my good friends. I can also invite refugees into the community of faith. I've often extended invitations to my refugee friends to attend church with me or attend other churches in our community.

And I can try to make my country a better place for them. Caring about our neighbors—who include refugees—involves caring about the systems and structures in which they live. We should be using our voices to speak up for refugees to our elected officials. As you attend town halls or look up the policy positions of your elected officials, ask what their position is on welcoming refugees to your community, and ask them to make public statements in support of refugees. World Relief and the Evangelical Immigration Table often have opportunities for people to sign letters and petitions supporting refugees, and they run specific campaigns throughout the year for people to get involved in supporting refugees.

But whether or not we succeed in influencing policy, every Christian is still able to love the stranger. We are inundated daily with facts and statistics about the refugee crisis, but we need to recognize that this issue is not just about the *millions* of displaced people, but also about that *one* person whom you or I may meet. Nader is one such person. His wife, Ramya, is another.

The "other" can become a friend, just as the Kassab family are friends to me and my family. Through my relationships with refugees, I have realized that there is indeed a difference between caring about something and caring for someone. My work involves caring about global poverty. But I am also to care for the individuals around me. When I have befriended refugees where I live in Baltimore, I have experienced generous hospitality, genuine friendship, and lots of laughter. In refugees' stories I have heard about extraordinary resilience and gratitude, born out of suffering and loss. In these interactions, I receive more than I'm able to give.

Jesus taught us to love radically, unconditionally, and sacrificially. People of different religions or cultures or ethnicities are not our enemies but individuals with whom we're supposed to build friendship and community as tangible expressions of our faith. The real enemy is fear. "Do not be afraid" is an oft-repeated command in the Bible. We must watch out and make sure that fear of others and a desire for an uninterrupted comfortable life do not prevent us from participating in the mission of God.

The stories of refugees can deepen our understanding of how God uses migration as part of his sovereign plan to bring people to himself. The church should be at the center of this story which God is weaving through the migration of people. When we choose, despite fear and discomfort, to love and welcome someone the world hates, people will concretely understand the reconciling work that Jesus did on the cross for *all* people.

8. CONVERSATIONS ON RACE

NATASHA SISTRUNK ROBINSON
AND LILLY PARK

DIVERSITY AND THE CHURCH: LILLY

A few years ago, at a church I was visiting, the pastor used an illustration for humor which was racially insensitive. It wasn't explicitly offensive, but it was unhelpful. The pastor simply was not aware of how others would receive his words.

That's partly why the church would benefit from wise conversations about race. Like that pastor, Christians—particularly those who come from the dominant culture—are not always aware of the effects of their own words and actions. Unfortunately, sometimes, we simply don't care enough to find out.

Even if we *do* know what *not* to say, is that enough? No, it isn't. Rather than avoiding the topic of race, we need to speak and listen carefully to one another and most importantly to God's word. Why? Because it would not be extreme to say that our approach to the topic of race affects the unity of the church and our testimony of Christ.

Diversity is God's idea, not our own. Jesus commands us to make disciples—of all nations (Matthew 28 v 19). Christians need to not only participate but take a lead in discussions on race, because we understand that God created each person in his image (Genesis 1 v 26-28) and that his kingdom is multi-ethnic (Revelation 7 v 9).

In the Bible, we see people from various ethnic, socio-economic, and geographical backgrounds work together to further God's kingdom. This happens in the Old Testament—think of Rahab or Ruth, non-Israelites who become part of God's people—but even more so in the New Testament. Jesus describes a hated Samaritan who is a better and kinder neighbor than those then admired in Jewish society (Luke 10 v 30-37); he heals a synagogue leader's dying daughter and a sick, poverty-stricken, ceremonially unclean woman on the same day (Mark 5 v 21-43); he admires the faith of a Roman centurion (Matthew 8 v 5-13). The ministry of the early church likewise included people from many ethnic groups and backgrounds (e.g. Acts 8 v 26-39; 10 v 1-48; 13 v 44-48).

But for Christians today it is not merely a question of trying to follow the example of Jesus and the early church. Our great hope is that we have been made one in Christ.

In Christ Jesus you are all sons of God, through faith. For as many of you as were baptized into Christ have put on Christ. There is neither Jew nor Greek, there is neither slave nor free, there is no male and female, for you are all one in Christ Jesus. (Galatians 3 v 26-28)

Christ breaks down walls of hostility and makes it possible for us to live at peace with those who are culturally different, just as he brought together previously separate Jews and Gentiles into one church (Ephesians 2 v 11-22). Whether we are gathering with other Christians in our homes and churches, or whether we are reaching out into our communities and our nation, we must bear witness to the power of the Holy Spirit at work within us, and to the Father's desire to unite us to himself and to each other.

It's not just about our own personal relationships and experiences, important though they are. It is about living as sanctified people in this world, chosen by God without regard to skin color, gender, or social status. We need to talk about racial issues not because of pragmatism ("It'll attract more people") or only because or morality ("It's the right thing to do"), but because unity in diversity reflects God's vision for the church.

The basis for our unity in Christ is our union with Christ. Paul asserts that "the same Lord is Lord of all" (Romans 10 v 12). There isn't a separate Christ for the majority-culture church, the black church, the Asian church, the Hispanic church, and so on. Yet that often seems to be our mentality about Christianity and race. *You do your own thing for God, and we'll do ours.*

But that's not how we'll spend eternity. One day we will stand before the throne, worshiping Jesus as part of a single great multitude "from every nation, from all tribes and peoples and languages" (Revelation 7 v 9). And we can start now.

Of course, diversity is not the purpose of the gospel nor the measure of success for a church. A multi-ethnic church is not necessarily more biblical than a church that is mostly white, black, Hispanic, Asian, or immigrant. But a church that is known for both biblical teaching and racial unity provides a beautiful glimpse of worship in heaven.

RACISM AND SOCIETY: NATASHA

We have to admit that this vision of unity in diversity can feel very far away from the society we live in.

I often compare racism to pollution. It is created by humans, it negatively impacts every one of us, and because it has been around for so long, we have become comfortable with its existence: so comfortable that some would deny it is even here.

In their classic book, *Divided by Faith: Evangelical Religion and the Problem of Race in America*, Christian sociologists

Michael O. Emerson and Christian Smith describe the American nation as a "racialized society." They write:

> *"A racialized society is a society wherein race matters profoundly for differences in life experiences, life opportunities, and social relationships. A racialized society can also be said to be 'a society that allocates differential economic, political, social, and even psychological rewards to groups along racial lines; lines that are socially constructed.'"* (page 7)

God has given us ethnic and cultural differences, which are not for the purposes of division, yet that is the exact purpose of the social construct of race. Race is a defining part of our society—affecting basic things such as where we live, as well as educational achievement and financial prospects.[1] The racializing of America's society has a long and often neglected history. The idea of race as division was the seed planted in America's soil which birthed the trees that bore the fruit of racism. This fruit is tilled, fertilized, and replanted throughout generations, until we look up one day to realize that there is a whole forest around us with tall trees entrapping us all, making it hard to see the light.

In 2012, CNN released a report which stated that children are learning racist thought processes in their homes—and then expressing them—when they are as young as six years old. They start becoming aware of racialized attitudes as young as five. The report stated that "making friends with kids of other races is hard, and only gets harder as they grow up."[2]

The problem does not start with children. The Public Religion Research Institute has reported that the majority of white Americans have very few non-white friends,[3] and are very unlikely to have intimate relationships with non-white people—the type of relationships in which they have important conversations or consider the person trustworthy.[4] If their parents' friends are all of one skin color, it should not be surprising that children find engaging with individuals from other people groups hard.

We all have an implicit bias: that is, our thoughts and actions are based on assumptions that we have been trained in since childhood and that we are not even aware of making. Because they are subconscious, these assumptions are the easiest to adopt unwittingly, and the hardest to identify or correct once they have taken root in our hearts. When unchallenged, such implicit biases have a profound effect not only on our own relationships but on those of our kids, and therefore on the society at large and on our collective future.

I was struck by the perspective shared by Patricia Raybon in her foreword to Amy Julia Becker's book *White Picket Fences*. Mrs. Raybon is an African American woman and a wise Christian writer. She is a product of the civil-rights movement and the Jim Crow era. She is also a mother of black children. All this came into the conversations she had with Amy Julia—a white woman—about race and privilege. Mrs. Raybon wrote:

> "She and I went back and forth on when to tell children about hard things such as racism. I argued that the question itself is a luxury allotted to children who don't have to worry about this particular terror—while children of color, by default, are forced to see from their earliest months that they are targets, often, of many kinds of racism.
>
> Thus, all children, I argued, should see that racial terror exists—just as they're taught that a stove is hot, a speeding car can kill them, and sadly so can other mayhem. Racism kills, too, and all children, no matter how young, should know about it."   (page xviii)

As a black mother, daughter, sister, wife, and friend, I know this trauma that does not escape us. But not everyone knows it. That is why talking about these things, however painful, is vitally important for unity and for the preservation of life.

As Christians, we must awaken ourselves to how God calls us to live for him in this world that is so drastically broken. We all need to consider how to prevent ourselves from inadvertently picking up those "racialized" seeds and planting them again.

Many people of color are tired of speaking up about race. Others are afraid to do so. Some people in our society are confused, and others frustrated; some simply feel they don't know what to say. The temptation for all of us is to remain silent.

But if we are to challenge a racialized society, we need to speak. We all need to be honest about the ways in which racism impacts and affects us. We need to confess and challenge the implicit bias that directs our actions and our words. We must look at ourselves and seek the truth about how our lack of knowledge, history, or understanding, and our silence, anger, or apathy prevent the message of Jesus Christ from going forth to all people.

BECOMING AWARE: LILLY

The need for honesty is urgent for us all because racism is a spiritual problem: a sin. We sin when we allow our personal preferences to trump God's standards in how we should relate to other people, valuing ourselves more than God's purposes and more than any love for our neighbors. This sinfulness is at the heart of racism, which views people who look different than us as being of lesser value than people who are similar to us. Racism displays our desire for more of "me."

But if we are seeking to serve the God who has saved us, we need to confess our sin of pride, arrogance, partiality, and more. If we confess our sin, God is faithful to forgive us

(1 John 1 v 9). And then we ask for his help in grasping—and acting upon—his love for all nations.

We can all ask questions of ourselves. Are you too selective in whom you greet or meet for meals, whether in the workplace, church, or school? Are you afraid of the unfamiliar, so that you don't say hello to new people or ask honest questions?

Often, it's apathy that robs us of the richness of connecting with people outside our circle of comfort and familiarity. Sometimes it's active dislike of certain people that hinders us from obeying God. Or it may be fear of the response we'll receive when we reach out to others.

There are simple ways of training ourselves to engage with people who seem "too different."

Try reading books or watching movies on cross-cultural issues or stories. These both teach us cultural differences and remind us of what is common to us all as human beings, breaking down the assumptions about people which can so often prevent us from building relationships with them. Such stereotypes are imperfect and reinforce implicit bias. We need to recognize that although all of us are part of a particular group or community, each individual also has a unique life story.

There is hope as we learn to listen well and ask thoughtful questions. We run the risk of speaking clumsily, but we can learn from our mistakes. We can ask others for help in learning where we have gone wrong in what we are saying or doing.

I know one interracial couple who, at first, experienced disapproval from the woman's parents. But they were Christians, and eventually they accepted the man who would become their son-in-law. As they got to know him, they realized that he was a godly man who loved their daughter. They repented of judging him based on the color of his skin and changed the way they thought and acted. I hope that we may all see this kind of repentance and reconciliation across our church and in wider society.

Earlier I gave an example of a pastor who had gotten it wrong, but church leaders can also play a significant positive role. As church members we can encourage our leaders to take race into account in church by addressing questions, sharing stories, and interacting with people from various backgrounds. Our leaders, by their example, can convey to listening ears and watching eyes that talking about race is meaningful. Perhaps then the whole church may develop a biblical perspective on what it means that we are all humans created in the image of God.

Change takes time. When I have seen good progress in a church or organization, a lot of conversations occurred before major decisions. Leaders wanted to understand the struggles, frustrations, and desires of the church members or fellow staff. They didn't speak to their inner circles only, but involved people who differed from them, and listened. I have met men and women who have been patient for years as they have discussed race in their ministry contexts. This feels frustrating, but it can lead to real progress. It happens one conversation at a time.

We won't single-handedly remove every societal barrier in the world, but each one of us can hope to contribute something to this conversation. For true change, the gospel has to be our motivation and purpose. So we must pray that God will help us and use us to make a difference for his glory. We must ask him to help us to keep the message of salvation central—and to take it to all people.

BECOMING ADVOCATES: NATASHA

There is an old saying which encourages us to have "a Bible in one hand and a newspaper in the other." Too often we have a newspaper in one hand and a Twitter feed in the other.

The media can shape our responses to racism and the solutions we endorse. But as Christians we need to respond to media stories concerning racism in a biblical way.

How do we allow the Bible to shape our thinking on this issue? It is important that we pay attention to the voices that are present in each Bible passage, asking who is speaking and from what perspective. This will help us to understand any injustice or marginalization that is taking place as the Bible describes sinful people and their attitudes. An astute Bible student often asks, "What does the word say?" but the fact that Jesus came to earth also enables us to consider, "What does the Word do?" How does Jesus respond to the vulnerable—including the poor, orphans, women, children, strangers, those in prison, and unbelievers? What is his attitude and why? Prayerfully asking these questions under the inspiration and guidance of the Holy Spirit will, I hope, lead us to greater compassion, wisdom, and understanding.

This, in turn, will help us respond to news stories with an informed, biblical viewpoint, and can also help us become wise, active advocates locally, nationally, and beyond. Rather than just responding to what's trending, we can consistently show a genuine pursuit of racial justice and a love for our neighbors. To do this, we can seek out, follow, learn from, and actively support the churches and organizations that are doing important work both in our local communities and nationally. It is also important that we read and listen to Christian witnesses who are people of color that are committed to the Bible, the good news of the gospel message, and justice work.

In this way we can all become advocates against racism. We can prayerfully shape our world so that it looks like the one we are ultimately looking forward to: a world in which people from every nation, tribe, people, and language will worship together before the throne of God, united eternally.

PART THREE

SPEAKING WELL

SPEAKING WELL:

INTRODUCTION TO PART 3

LINDSAY NICOLET

God created humans in his image. This means that we can contribute to our culture for his glory by reflecting and representing him in whatever ways we can. One way we do this is through what we say and how we speak, because he is a God of words. By his words he brought everything into existence and continues to uphold creation. And by his gospel word he calls the dead to eternal life.

As we see throughout the Bible, the Lord has entrusted women with speaking powerful and precious things in winsome and wise ways—things that he used to turn their culture upside down.

In the Old Testament, Abigail's wise words kept David from committing sin (1 Samuel 25). And Esther's words of courage helped preserve the Jewish people (Esther 7 – 8).

In the New Testament, teenage Mary proclaimed obediently, "Behold, I am the servant of the Lord; let it be to me according to your word" (Luke 1 v 38). Mary Magdalene, after finding Jesus alive at his tomb, announced the unbelievable news to the frightened disciples (John 20 v 17-18). And Lois and Eunice, Timothy's grandmother and mom, used their words to pass on their sincere faith (2 Timothy 1 v 5).

On the other hand, women in the Bible also caused great destruction with their words. Eve encouraged Adam to sin (Genesis 3). Sarai urged Abram to sleep with Hagar (Genesis 16). Rebekah concocted Jacob's deception of Isaac (Genesis 27). And I imagine there were women among the crowd before Jesus, crying out, "Let him be crucified!" (Matthew 27 v 22).

Can you, like me, relate to these women? My words have sometimes revealed my heart to be holy and at other times to be wicked. I have used my words to persuade people for good and bad, to build up and tear down, to point to Christ and to point to myself. I have used them to proclaim the gospel and to misrepresent it. I need the Lord's help to be a woman who speaks well, bringing life, hope, and gospel change to the people in the culture around me. What about you?

The Lord is calling us, as Christian women, to steward our words well, just as he did our mothers in the faith. Yet ours is an age in which this extends to the words we type and text too. Our words should be salt and light, agents of good news and change in our churches, communities, families, and social-media spheres. Women have more influence than we often realize, although we don't all fit the same mold. The Lord has given some of us an audience with lawmakers who can affect big issues like abortion or marriage; others have the responsibility of discipling children through mundane interruptions and tantrums; others can seek regular interactions with widowed neighbors, local hair-stylists, or cashiers at the grocery store. Our communication in all these areas has a lasting impact, either shepherding people toward our Savior or away from his call.

There are two ways in which we can shape our relationships and environments. First, we can hurt or heal with the substance of our speech. We should speak true, gracious, and wise words. We're called to encourage, not tear down; unite, not divide; give thanks, not complain; and promote purity, not what's filthy. This applies in a thousand ways.

Second, *how* we speak is just as important as what we say. Our tone matters. That tweet thread may be accurate, but if it belittles another's dignity in how we word it, it's better not to post it. We can share the gospel with our combative family members, but if we're yelling the whole time, we're just a noisy gong. We need more winsomeness amid the chatter and a way of communicating that demonstrates a heart of love.

If there's one thing our 21st-century Western society has trouble with, it's speaking well. Whether it's seen in the talking head on a news channel, the viral thread that shows up on our feeds, the heated discussion next to us in the coffee shop, or the spiteful comments left on the latest mom blog, ours is a divisive and polarized age. Many around us can't seem to talk—or tweet—calmly, rationally, and respectfully with those who hold differing viewpoints.

This gives Christians a unique opportunity to be beautifully distinct as we bring the message of Jesus into a world desperate for a life-giving narrative. The chapters in this section will give you practical ways to do this. The authors serve as your cheerleaders, supporting you as you seek to speak Jesus-soaked words into areas often polluted by sin and in need of sanctification. First, we look at the world of social media, with all its traps and opportunities; then the specific topic of beauty, which can be so hard to speak about in a biblical way; and finally, your own story, and how it can be used to speak about the best news of all—the gospel of Jesus Christ.

At this specific time in history, let's take the opportunity to be wise women who weigh our words and use them to adorn the gospel. No, we can't do this on our own. But with God's grace and power, we can follow in the footsteps of Abigail,

Esther, Mary, and Lois, who paved the path for the good news of Jesus in ways they couldn't foresee. Let's speak wise words of truth in a winsome and gracious way so as to show the beauty of our God and remove any stumbling blocks that would keep ears from hearing the distinct voice of our Savior.

9. SURFING THE
SOCIAL-MEDIA WAVE

ERIN DAVIS

What if Jesus preached the Sermon on the Mount in your community today? The message wouldn't need to be overhauled. We still need to hear about anger, anxiety, and living like salt and light. His delivery wouldn't need to be tweaked or modified. What *would* have changed is the way the listener listens. Just about everyone gathered to hear Jesus preach would be holding a smartphone or tablet. Some would record the entire sermon on their device. Others would shoot selfies of themselves with Jesus in the background to blast out on social media. Instead of hearing Christ's words as a call to change their lives, they might simply feel a tug toward fleeting hashtag activism: #thegoldenrule.

Social media has dramatically shifted the ways people today engage with truth and with each other. Screens are here to stay, and over-romanticizing life without screens won't help us hold onto truth more tightly. (How did Jesus keep all those kids from melting down without YouTube Kids, anyway? A true miracle.) Instead of fighting the social-media tide, we must learn to surf it.

Though time has branded this most famous sermon "The Sermon on the Mount," we could just as easily call it

"The Sermon of the Heart." Jesus captivated his original listeners, and captivates believers still, by addressing the deep issues of our hearts. Anger, generosity, lust—these issues do not go away, however much the world changes.

It was also in this sermon that Jesus gave his followers our identity as salt and light.

> *You are the salt of the earth, but if salt has lost its taste, how shall its saltiness be restored? It is no longer good for anything except to be thrown out and trampled under people's feet.*
>
> *You are the light of the world. A city set on a hill cannot be hidden. Nor do people light a lamp and put it under a basket, but on a stand, and it gives light to all in the house. In the same way, let your light shine before others, so that they may see your good works and give glory to your Father who is in heaven.*
>
> *(Matthew 5 v 13-16)*

Social media has expanded the borders of our "city." We now have as access to people across the street, across the country, and around the world with a single click. So how do we steward this unique opportunity? If the church is to be a beacon of gospel hope in the digital age, what cautions should we heed? As I consider my own desire to use social media to fulfill Christ's calling to be salt and light, I let the following principles guide what I click, like, and post.

Social media is a magnifying glass. It is value neutral. At the end of the day, social media is just software. Yet it magnifies or highlights what is already in our hearts, homes, and churches.

Therefore, as we consider our social-media habits, we are wise to consider Christ's words: "The good person out of the good treasure of his heart produces good, and the evil person out of his evil treasure produces evil, for out of the abundance of the heart his mouth speaks"—or tweets, as the case may be (Luke 6 v 45). This verse makes me pause and consider my output, owning the fact that what I send out through my feeds is a reflection of the true condition of my heart.

Meanwhile, Proverbs 4 v 23 helps me consider my input— the messages I'm allowing to flow *into* my heart through my laptop and phone screens: "Keep your heart with all vigilance, for from it flow the springs of life." We see throughout Scripture that while God cares for us as whole people, he is most concerned about our hearts (see 1 Samuel 16 v 7; Mark 12 v 28-34). We need to be vigilant about what we allow into our hearts, as well as being aware of what comes out of them and whether it is godly and good.

Social media impacts our actions and interactions. As Christ-followers who want to be faithful, we must dig deeper, past the surface of clicks and likes. How does social media reveal what's in our *hearts*?

1. LIVING TO PLEASE

Every Facebook like, Twitter share, and Instagram heart has an effect on our brains. They are hits, giving the brain a tiny shot of the feel-good chemical dopamine. One study among teenagers revealed that social-media likes activate the same part of the brain that lights up when they eat chocolate or win money.[1] All of us, young or old, are prone to an addictive cycle of seeking this chemical "high" more and more. Because of our biology, we face a real temptation to post, and live, for likes.

This science is worth noting because Scripture warns us plainly, "The fear of man lays a snare, but whoever trusts in the LORD is safe" (Proverbs 29 v 25). When we live and serve to please people instead of God, we will find ourselves desperately entangled. That's always been true, but the mechanism we are trapped by has changed.

This is as much a danger for Christians seeking to use social media to serve God as it is for anyone else. We can measure our ministry by Facebook analytics. We can gauge our effectiveness by shares. We can receive immediate feedback on every Bible idea we post. Yet God does not call us to measure our kingdom work by these markers. He has told us what is good:

> *And what does the LORD require of you*
> *but to do justice, and to love kindness,*
> *and to walk humbly with your God? (Micah 6 v 8)*

Paul confirms that we are to do these things for the long haul, rather than expecting results all at once:

> *And let us not grow weary of doing good, for in due*
> *season we will reap, if we do not give up.*
> *(Galatians 6 v 9)*

These commands are not flashy. They won't go viral. They take commitment, integrity, grit, and grace by the bucketful.

I said before that social media works like a magnifying glass over what's already in our hearts. It is wise to pay attention to what social media exposes about our fear of others and craving for affirmation.

Our craving for acceptance is part of our wiring. The answer isn't to live our lives unconcerned by what anyone thinks of us, but rather to find our identity first and foremost in who God says that we are: to make a daily habit of turning first toward him to satisfy our craving for acceptance.

I've wrestled with setting my heart on the right trajectory in this area. If I wake up and turn to my phone, I will spend the day chasing the high of likes and follows. If, instead, I turn my attention first to God's word, to his character, I find that my tank is filled. The affirmation of others becomes a secondary bonus, not the primary motivator for my behavior for the day.

2. LONGING FOR CONNECTION

Because of social media, the young people sitting beside you in church are more connected than any generation before them. They're quite possibly lonelier too. Their average of 243 Facebook friends aren't translating into real-life friendships. Researchers theorize that we are spending so much time online that we no longer have capacity to spend time with our non-Facebook friends.[2]

One young woman recently told me that WhatsApp has become a hindrance to her relationships with people within her own zip code.

"Faraway friends and family can easily get in contact via internet messaging, and sometimes it really does feel that there is so much pressure to be in touch with people in that way that there is less time to hang out with the people who I am actually geographically close to," she said.

"Skin hunger"—the need for physical human contact—is a real condition that is impacting more and more of us. Think of skin hunger as the adult version of failure to thrive; the result is that we are emotionally undernourished and struggling to grow in our relationships.

One study discovered that, for the first time ever, young people are as lonely as the elderly—the group typically seen as the loneliest among us.[3] When a generation that is generally active, mobile and well-connected is facing the same chronic and debilitating loneliness that the often isolated or physically limited elderly face, something has clearly gone awry.

Beyond being a burden for us to carry, this spreading epidemic of loneliness poses larger risks. It's easier for people to hide within the church, meaning it's easier for their sin to stay hidden. The enemy often attacks the isolated with deception. Without the safety net of meaningful connections with other believers, we become easy prey.

Social media also affords us the illusion of connecting with others without the need to actually invest in people's lives. Sure, post an encouraging note on a wall. Respond to that DM, but don't allow those to be replacements for God's call to teach, to feed, to pray, to care for and to live in the trenches with other believers.

If we're honest, we know our "iStuff" isn't satisfying our craving to know and be known. In a way, this is good news! Christians have something better to offer.

> But now ... you have come to know God, or rather be
> known by God.   (Galatians 4 v 9)

He knows us, and he knows what we need. It is in Christ, and in the body of Christ, that we should seek the connection we long for.

3. NEEDING TO REST

Most adults spend at least eight to twelve hours per day staring at screens. That's more time than we spend on any other activity, including sleeping.[4] No wonder we're totally exhausted. Personally, I've had seasons of enduring a phenomenon I call "sacred deprivation"—a feeling of bone-weary exhaustion that stems not from lack of sleep but rather from lack of margin.

For too many of us, there's no slot on our calendar that is set apart. We are accessible every moment. We're not sure how to enjoy the Sabbath rest God calls us to.

There is a solution so simple that we may have missed it. It's the little on/off button on the side of our phones and in the corner of our laptops. If we do not figure out how to unplug (literally), we will find ourselves perpetually depleted.

The first problem with not resting from social media is that we're overloaded with people interactions. But there is a second, more dangerous problem. When we never take a break from our feeds, we become overloaded with images and stories, and thus desensitized to need and sin.

Our eyeballs are so inundated with images and stories and pleas relayed through social media that we are forced to numb our empathetic response in order to avoid system overload. We've lost the ability to be shocked. Yet human brokenness should shock us often, working like a defibrillator, which causes pain but brings life. Being aware of human need and sin hurts, but it also brings us back to our desperate need for a savior.

4. UNFAMILIAR WITH THE WORD

As social-media use rockets upward, there's another trend we need to pay attention to—the nosedive of Biblical literacy among modern Christians. Here are some stats.[5] I'll warn you: they're jarring.

- Fewer than half of all adults can name the four Gospels.
- Many Christians cannot identify more than two or three of the Gospels.
- 60% of Americans can't name even five of the Ten Commandments.
- According to 82% of Americans, "God helps those who help themselves" is a Bible verse. (Those who identified as born-again Christians scored better by only 1%.)
- Over 50% of graduating seniors in one survey thought that Sodom and Gomorrah were husband and wife.

The reasons for the scandal of Biblical illiteracy are numerous and varied, but there is one very simple obvious cause: when we're spending up to twelve hours per day on our screens, we no longer have time to open up God's word.

But there's another way that this problem shows itself, and it's more subtle.

Modern Christians have access to sermons and teachings 24 hours a day. We can sleep in on Sunday and catch a sermon on podcast while we mow the lawn. We scroll through feeds filled with Bible quotes and Christian music videos.

It might sound like a good thing that modern technology allows so much teaching to come straight into our homes. Yet so much of what is sharable isn't helpful or rooted in the authority of Scripture.

It is wise for us to regularly evaluate the messages entering our hearts through our earbuds. Do the voices that come up on your feed hold high the banner of God's truth or are they just presenting their own ideas?

I can listen to sermons in my car, pull up an article on applying God's word from my desk at work, and scroll through discussions about theological ideas while I wait for my kids in the car line. Simply because we're all so accessible, there is more of an infiltration of wolves among the sheep—false teachers who have the appearance of wisdom (see Matthew 7 v 15)—that in many ways is unprecedented. There may not be more wolves among us (Christ's message has always had many opponents), but could it be that we are listening to their howling more often?

Instead, we must remind each other that God's word is the plumb line for truth and authority in our lives. Let's not be covert about it. The risks are too high, and the voices too many. Let's make it a point to regularly challenge one another to take everything we're reading, listening to, and sharing, and squeeze it through the grid of God's word.

I'm not talking about passive-aggressively posting Bible verses on each other's Facebook walls. Hearts and minds are rarely won through Twitter spats. There are gentler ways to hold high the banner of God's word in these days. We can…

- post our words less often and God's word more often.
- commit to following others who we know will point us to Jesus and his word.
- share frequently specific ways in which God's word is transforming our own hearts and homes.

As we do these things, we will be letting God's powerful word speak for itself.

OUR UNIQUE OPPORTUNITY

Social media certainly exposes the darkness that exists in our broken world. We're all just a few clicks away from stories of depravity and loss. It also reveals the depths of our own hearts, which often wander far from the Lord. But where darkness is deepest, light shines even more.

Everyone with a smartphone can declare the goodness of the Lord to "the ends of the earth" (Psalm 22 v 27). While there are challenges, there is also a unique opportunity to broadcast our gospel hope.

This must be our focus as we seek to be Christ's followers in a social media world. Instead of simply villainizing, grumbling about, or refusing to address social media (for fear of receiving a virtual thumbs down), let us take the challenges and opportunities of our times and hold them up to the timeless truth God has gifted us in his word.

10. WHAT WE SAY
ABOUT BEAUTY

JEN WILKIN

I recently came across an article showing ads from the 1930s and '40s selling products to help people gain weight. The ads made claims that sound completely comical to our ears:

"Add 5lb of solid flesh in a week!"

"Since I gained 10lb I have all the dates I want!"

I showed the ads to my daughters, whose response was "Mom, those must be made up."

But they're real all right, despite how preposterous they seem. For much of human history, the curvy beauty has prevailed. Statues of women from ancient Greece and Rome celebrate a body type we would call "plus-size" today, as does Renaissance art. Historically, padded women were considered beautiful because only the rich and idle could achieve such a figure, and because curviness indicated fertility. For women of past generations, curviness was extremely hard to achieve unless you had the money to eat well and work little. Thanks to trans fats and high-fructose corn syrup, this is no longer the case. To many, slimness is the new ideal: the rich and idle of today strive to look undernourished and overworked, and the rest of us rush to follow suit.

So, would it have been better to have lived during a time when well-fed women were hailed as beauties? I doubt it—because the issue is not "fat versus thin"; it is "perfect versus imperfect." Even when we are encouraged to stop thinking about weight and seek strength over skinniness, the underlying message is the same: there is an ideal body, and you don't have it.

There has never been a time when women have not defined themselves by some ideal of physical beauty. There has never been a time when women have not believed that this ideal exists and should be pursued at all costs. Though its definition may change across the centuries, one element remains constant: it is always just beyond our reach. We want what we cannot have. If curvy is hard to achieve, we want curvy. If thin is hard to achieve, we want thin. We long to be beautiful—whatever our culture tells us "beautiful" means—and we spend a great deal of time trying to achieve it.

In our culture, physical "perfection" is the legacy of womanhood, handed down with meticulous care from mother to daughter, with faithful instruction in word and deed. It is the constant subject of conversation between girlfriends. It is the center of our worries. It is the focus of our compliments, so that even when we are trying to encourage and uplift one another, we often unintentionally reinforce the idea that pursuing physical perfection is a good goal.

Surely we can find a better approach. Surely we can find a better way of talking about beauty.

THE TRUTH ABOUT OUR BODIES

Our culture tells us a series of lies about how we should perceive our bodies. But we can look to Scripture to examine these lies and help ourselves to shift our perspective.

The first lie we are told is about ownership. To whom does your body belong? Western culture says your body belongs to you. You are its owner. You may neglect it, obsess over it, indulge it, punish it, pamper it, or alter it as you wish. The choice is yours, and the consequences will be yours alone to savor or suffer.

But the Bible says that your body is not yours.

> *Or do you not know that your body is a temple of the Holy Spirit within you, whom you have from God? You are not your own, for you were bought with a price. So glorify God in your body.*
> *(1 Corinthians 6 v 19-20)*

You are the steward of your body, not the owner. Because you were bought with a price, all decisions about and behaviors toward your body must be run through the filter of the question "Does this glorify God in my body?" In other words, does the way I treat my body help me to love God and others or hinder me from doing that? Decisions about our bodies never impact us alone.

The second lie we are told is about purpose. What is your body for? We are told by our culture that our bodies are decorative: useful for attracting the attention of men and the envy of women. The body can and should be trained, toned, and preserved from all signs of aging. What matters most is how it looks, because its level of attractiveness—or, as we've been told in more recent years, its strength—can and should be leveraged to give you dominance over and independence from others.

But Scripture says that what matters most about the body is not how it looks but what it does. The body is useful, created to do good works which serve God.

> *For we are his workmanship, created in Christ Jesus*
> *for good works, which God prepared beforehand, that*
> *we should walk in them.*   *(Ephesians 2 v 10)*

And instead of telling us to focus on preserving our strength and youth, the Bible points out that our bodies are fragile and fleeting (Isaiah 40 v 6-8, 23-24, 30; Romans 8 v 20-23). Our bodies bear the impact of the fall. People who face challenges such as disability, disfigurement, infertility, chronic illness, terminal illness and advanced age think of their bodies differently than people who don't. They tend to enjoy a heightened ability to value wellness over attractiveness. They readily understand that a beautiful body is a body that simply functions as it should.

The third lie we are told is about alterations. How might we improve on what we've got? We are told by Western culture that our appearance is flawed but fixable. You are not the right size, shape, or color, but you can and should go to enormous effort and expense to change that. Our culture tells us that what we should be hoping for is a better body, and eventually a perfect body. By making these physical changes, you can change the condition of your heart. Once you look right, you will have more self-confidence, better self-esteem, and greater happiness.

But the truth is that your body's appearance was planned by God. You were purposefully knitted together by him in your mother's womb (Psalm 139 v 13). Because God is a God of infinite creativity, people come in many different sizes, shapes and colors. While our bodies are not "perfect" in the sense that our culture demands, they are designed by a perfect God.

Not only this, but our bodies have a glorious future. There is a type of physical perfection that we can achieve. It will be reached in heaven.

So it is with the resurrection of the dead. What is sown is perishable; what is raised is imperishable. It is sown in dishonor; it is raised in glory. It is sown in weakness; it is raised in power. It is sown a natural body; it is raised a spiritual body.

(1 Corinthians 15 v 42-44)

This is true hope and good news for the believer: one day we will be free of our self-loathing and will live in harmony with our physical appearance. We will be given new, incorruptible bodies—bodies that are no longer on a collision course with the grave.

We dare not reduce this future hope to that of an eternity with thinner thighs or a smaller nose. We must celebrate it as the day when vanity itself is dealt a fatal and final blow.

IN THE MEANTIME

We can lay claim now to this future hope. Every time we look in the mirror and are tempted to complain, we could say instead, "Your kingdom come, your will be done, on earth as it is in heaven" (Matthew 6 v 10)—accepting that our bodies are imperfect and fragile, acknowledging that they are designed, created, and owned by God, and looking forward to the day when they will be made perfect with him in glory.

And then we can strive to live in the light of these truths. We can labor to live in right relation to our bodies now instead of only at the resurrection.

By all means, seek to steward the gift of your physical body. We should present our bodies as living sacrifices, ready to work in accordance with God's will. That means caring for our bodies—but for the sake of wellness, not beauty. Two women can step onto two treadmills with identical fitness goals and widely different motives. Only they will know the real reason why they are there.

1 Peter 3 v 3-4 is often quoted to encourage women not to focus too much on their appearance.

> *Do not let your adorning be external—the braiding of hair and the putting on of gold jewelry, or the clothing you wear—but let your adorning be the hidden person of the heart with the imperishable beauty of a gentle and quiet spirit, which in God's sight is very precious.*

But is Peter's purpose to tell us that we should never do anything to make ourselves look nice? No. In this passage he is speaking to wives with unbelieving husbands, regarding how they might seek to win them for Christ. He contrasts the influence of their outward beauty with the influence of their inward beauty. He's saying, *Are you relying on something that is perishable when you have something imperishable to rely on?* Rather than a warning against adornments, this is an instruction about the power of inward beauty to draw others to Christ.[1]

There is nothing wrong with wanting to look our best, insofar as doing so does not begin to absorb excessive time, thought, effort, or expense. But what our culture calls physical "perfection" is not within our grasp—nor should it be what we are aiming for. The common marketing pitch that transforming the outside will fix the way we feel on the inside is a lie. It is an inversion (and a perversion) of the good news, which promises transformation in an opposite direction. The believer's hope is that transformation on the inside enables us to make peace with the outside.

> *I appeal to you therefore, brothers, by the mercies of God, to present your bodies as a living sacrifice, holy and acceptable to God, which is your spiritual worship. Do not be conformed to this world, but be transformed by the renewal of your mind, that by*

*testing you may discern what is the will of God, what
is good and acceptable and perfect.*

(Romans 12 v 1-2)

A mind being progressively transformed by the gospel rejects
the worship of self and the futile pursuit of happiness. By pursuing holiness instead, our attitudes toward our bodies will
change as we learn to love them as instruments, as good gifts
from God. We can have healthy confidence because we have
confidence in God, and because we are laying up treasure in
heaven, which can never be destroyed.

What if we began to build a legacy of womanhood that cele-
brates character over carb-avoidance and godliness over glamor?
What if we simply didn't talk so much about calories, work-
outs and weight loss? What if we didn't talk about body sizes at
all? What if we made it a point not to mention our own calorie
sins or victories in front of our girlfriends and daughters?

Sure—hit the gym, eat the Paleo diet, run six miles a day,
wear Spanx from neck to knee; but just stop talking about it.
Stop telling your friend she looks slim; instead tell her you love
her sweet spirit. Choose compliments that spur her to pursue
that which lasts instead of that which certainly does not. If
someone comments on your own shape, say thanks and change
the subject. Banish body-talk to the same list of off-limits topics
as salaries, name-dropping, and colonoscopies. Apply the discipline you use to work out to controlling your tongue.

But whatever you do, don't avoid bestowing the
compliment of "beautiful".

A BETTER "BEAUTIFUL"

I grew up with a dad who told me I was beautiful—a lot. I
would roll my eyes as he'd say it, reaching out to hug me,
and I would think to myself, "He just thinks that because he's
my dad." My subscription to *Seventeen* magazine reminded

me faithfully every month that I was not, in fact, beautiful at all. My hair was stick-straight (a debilitating handicap for '80s hair). I had a bad complexion. I had the shoulder span of a linebacker in an era when giant shoulder pads were routinely added to women's shirts, seemingly for the sole purpose of enhancing my freakishness. I was no curvier than the 13-year-old boys I desperately hoped would ask me to dance, even as I loomed over them with my gargantuan height. Clearly, my dad was delusional.

But he was the best kind of delusional. He was the kind of delusional every daughter needs. He saw something in me that the mirror didn't, and he routinely and faithfully pronounced me beautiful regardless of all external measures.

We become more beautiful in the knowing. Which of us has not met someone whom we at first thought to be plain, but whom upon longer acquaintance we grew to find beautiful? When we tell someone she is beautiful, what we mean is that she is beautiful to us. It is a way of telling someone that it is a sheer joy to know them.

This particularly applies to parents. In our image-driven culture, young girls already perceive their physical "flaws" to the point that the face value of the words "You're beautiful" will ring untrue. But, God willing, they will learn the deeper significance of these words because of who speaks them. Because we know our daughters better than any other human does, our opinion counts more than anyone else's. Our daughters will see how our belief in their beauty intertwines with our love for their person, and realize that they are valued just as they are. When every billboard and magazine cover and internet ad is telling your daughter that she is not beautiful, the knowledge that you absolutely, irrationally, vehemently disagree may just be the thing that keeps her heart whole.

But the benefits of saying "You're beautiful" extend beyond the parent-child relationship. When we tell our daughters—and our mothers, sisters, grandmothers and friends—that they are beautiful, we are modeling the love of a heavenly Father who "sees not as man sees" (1 Samuel 16 v 7). When we simply tell them they are beautiful—avoiding the poisonous language of complexion or color, of size or shape, of failure or perfection—we give them permission and power to measure beauty differently. We show them that it is possible to focus not merely on the outward appearance but on the heart.

LOOKING UP

Would it help us grow in godliness to readjust our language as we speak to one another about beauty? Yes. Would it help us grow in godliness to change our inward motivations and mantras and say no to the cultural lies that surround us every day? Yes. But the greatest help to having a healthy, godly, biblical view of our bodies is to think about something else altogether.

We so easily measure ourselves by a human standard instead of a divine one, succumbing to and revering human opinion as truth. But the ultimate antidote to the fear of people is the fear of God. We need to offer our reverence and awe to its true object: God himself.

You can tell me that I'm beautiful, truthfully and fervently. You can tell me that I am God's masterpiece, that I am sung over and delighted in, that I am beautiful in his eyes, that I am set apart for a sacred purpose. You can tell me these things, and you should. But I beg you, first tell me to gaze in awe at God. Though all of these statements are precious truths, their preciousness cannot be properly perceived until framed in the brilliance of his utter holiness.

In my book *None Like Him* (Crossway, 2016) I wrote about awe and what it means to fear the Lord:

"Research shows that when humans experience awe—wonderment at redwoods or rainbows, Rembrandt or Rachmaninoff—we become less individualistic, less self-focused, less materialistic, more connected to those around us. In marveling at something greater than ourselves, we become more able to reach out to others … Awe helps us worry less about self-worth by turning our eyes first toward God, then toward others. It also helps establish our self-worth in the best possible way: we understand both our insignificance within creation and our significance to our Creator." (pages 154-155)

When we consider the God who created the world and who embodies perfection, when we truly "worship the LORD in the splendor of holiness" (Psalm 96 v 9), when we glimpse something of what he is really like, we tremble and stammer, "Depart from me, for I am a sinful woman." On such holy ground, self-conscious thoughts of body image have no place. They are rightfully replaced with awe at the miracle of our acceptance through Christ.

To lift our eyes to the transcendent God is to reorient ourselves to true beauty, eternal beauty, unchanging beauty. The prophet Isaiah tells us that our beauty is as fragile as grass—and then suggests that that should lead us to submit to and depend on the strong and eternal God.

> *All flesh is grass,*
> *and all its beauty is like the flower of the field.*
> *The grass withers, the flower fades*
> *when the breath of the LORD blows on it;*
> *surely the people are grass.*
> *The grass withers, the flower fades,*
> *but the word of our God will stand forever.*
> (Isaiah 40 v 6b-8)

In Acts chapter 1, as the apostles watch Jesus ascend into the clouds and disappear from sight, two angelic messengers assure them:

> *Men of Galilee, why do you stand looking into heaven? This Jesus, who was taken up from you into heaven, will come in the same way as you saw him go into heaven.* (v 11)

This Jesus. This Jesus, in his resurrected body: "the firstfruits of those who have fallen asleep" (1 Corinthians 15 v 20). At this very moment, Jesus Christ sits at the right hand of the Father in a body of flesh. His resurrected body is a promise that our withering, fading flesh will one day, too, be raised incorruptible.

This is the reason to pursue the truth of Scripture instead of accepting the lies of our culture. This is the reason to look forward to that day, and to live in the light of that sure expectation. This is the reason to discipline our tongues and create a culture in which physical appearance has nothing to do with how much we value ourselves and one another.

We must fix our eyes upon Jesus, the One whose beauty will never, ever fade. In this captivating vision is found healthy self-forgetfulness, help for the weak, and hope eternal.

11. TELLING YOUR STORY

JACKIE HILL PERRY

Stories are powerful.

Think of the woman at the well. She meets Jesus when she goes to draw water and he asks her for a drink. Soon it's become clear to her that she, dried up by all her past mistakes and desperate for something or someone that will be good for her, needs him far more than he needs her and her little water jug. She has this conversation with Jesus in which she discovers that he knows all about her, and so she leaves her jug behind by the well, and she goes and tells all the people in her town about what he said. *Could this be the Messiah, could this be the prophet we've been waiting for?* she says to them (John 4 v 29). *He told me all that I ever did.*

This woman didn't need a theological education to declare the glory of Jesus, because he is theology. She met the Word himself, and he spoke about her own story. He knew her, and he knew what she needed. And so this woman went and told people about what had happened. They went straight to Jesus, and a few days later they were able to say to the woman, *We've seen for ourselves that what you are saying is true* (v 42).

That is a great example of evangelistic testimony telling, which is just telling folks about your encounter with Jesus. Any encounter with Jesus. It doesn't have to be your whole life story or the story of how you came to faith. It doesn't have to be super-complicated. It's a matter of discerning the relationships that you have, the conversations that you have, and finding little ways to talk about Jesus. It could be "Last week I had anxiety, but I cast my cares on him because he cares for me, and now I have peace." Though small, it is still your story. Talking about how Jesus met you when you were feeling overwhelmed is just as glorifying and powerful, and able to be used by the Holy Spirit as the telling of your conversion would be. Any story can be the starting point for telling *his* story too.

STORIES SHAPE US

Right now a lot of people are turning away from or changing their beliefs, not based on theology but based on compelling narratives that they've heard. Stories are literally shaping the way people think about God and sex and sin and money. While you may be able to discuss theology with a person who disagrees with you—and you should—it's a hard thing to argue with someone else's experience and someone else's story because everybody connects to pain and triumph, fear and courage, so when we listen to narratives about these things, we are prone to letting them shape the way we think.

When it is stories that are leading people away from God and away from his word, it is important for Christians to have a counter-narrative that will invite them back. And each of us has a story—each of us has countless stories—that can be that counter-narrative.

Let me explain by telling you my story and how I've told it. In the end it is not just my story but the story of Jesus and the good news of the gospel.

MY STORY

My story begins with me realizing when I was six or seven that I had same-sex desires. I didn't know the name for it.

It just was a feeling, something that I noticed in myself. It was when I went to church that I realized *This is homosexuality, and it seems like Christians don't like it too much.*

It was at high school that I decided that being a heterosexual was harder than just acting out on what I thought myself to be. So I became a lesbian, and I enjoyed it. It felt natural. It felt freeing. It felt like a better option for love. And then, when I was 19, God spoke to my heart. He showed me that his concern was not only my sexuality but my whole life. Christians had talked to me as if homosexuality was the only thing God wanted me to repent of. But through his Spirit he showed me: *No, Jackie, your whole heart is problematic.*

I saw that Jesus had to be the worthy one and the good one. And by his grace I chose him, and now I'm different. Different as in freed from the power of sin (Romans 6 v 22) and able to live for and love God. This was and is the hope of everyone who believes, gay or straight: that the God who will make all things new has come to do that in us.

That's my story, as far as it can be told in a few paragraphs. That's the story I've told again and again, and in one way it's your story too: *By his grace, now I'm different.*

I didn't like poetry before I became a Christian. I thought poetry was for really deep people. But when I was a new Christian, I had an uninitiated desire to write something. So I wrote a poem, because I figured that's what people do when they want to write something deep.

I was eventually invited to do a poem about my testimony at an event in Los Angeles. The poem was called "My Life as a Stud." In it I told my story, the story of how I had been and how God reached down in grace to save and change me. By God's sovereign hand, it eventually got significant traction on YouTube, which began my traveling ministry.

Through the poem, people were able to interact with the gospel. People that don't go to church, that don't trust pastors, that don't trust Christians watched the poem because they were unaware of how God can speak through art just as much as he can speak through a sermon. They might have been unwilling to meet with God through his people during a Sunday service, but poetry, a form of communication that God has used for centuries, offered them a counter-narrative: one revealing God's Son and challenging their own hearts.

LIVING STORIES

Art is like that, and so is any story we might tell that has God in it. People listen to it unguardedly, so it gives them glimpses of the glory of God that they might not otherwise see—like the heavens, which declare the glory of God (Psalm 19 v 1). God reveals himself in the things he has made, and art is one avenue in which we can reveal God with the things we make.

But just as poetry isn't only for those deep people, the glory of God isn't just to be left for the heavens to declare. *By his grace, now I'm different.* Those are words that tell of God's glory. And don't we all have a story like that?

My point is that you and I don't have to be able to write in a poetic form in order to tell our stories and share our testimonies. This is something all of us can do.

We're telling stories all day, anyway. Maybe you're telling the story to your neighbor about how your kid threw bananas on the floor. You're telling the story to your friend about how your husband didn't put the milk back in the fridge. You're telling the story to your mother about what your boss said to you at work that bothered you. We're always telling stories. And so speaking about God is really just finding a way to insert our story and his story into the common stories that we're telling and living all the time.

I saw that when I worked at a fast-food restaurant. I worked there for maybe six or seven years, and I knew that this was not merely a job. This was a place where God had put me.

The apostle Paul said that God "determined allotted periods and the boundaries of [everyone's] dwelling place, that they should seek God, and perhaps feel their way toward him and find him" (Acts 17 v 26-27). I was in that workplace, and the people I was working with were there, in order that I could show him off to them. And so I found opportunities and ways to speak about him.

A lot of those opportunities came by me living life a certain way. I was living with integrity. Then one time one of my co-workers said, "Jackie, what made you change? Because you're so different than us." And I was able to tell my story.

In a way it's a greater thing for me to do that than it is to share my story on a stage or online, because when I'm talking on stage or in a video, I'm talking to people, not with them. It's not truly intimate. The audience sees me divulging all of this information, and they may feel as if they're connected with me, but they don't really know my life in the way that my neighbor or coworker can who is with me every day. It's a greater thing to be able to build real, authentic relationships with people—off stage, away from social media—where they can see you as well as hear you.

You, too, may want to share your story on social media. Do it, as you feel led. You can even do it in a ten-word caption. *I used to be this, but now I am not.* That's a testimony. That's a story. It doesn't have all the flesh that eventually needs to be put on the bones, but it's enough to get a conversation started. But be careful: don't be taken in by a false sense of intimacy online. It may be easier and more convenient to type something than it is to look somebody in the face and say it, but be wise in how and what you say. Don't tell your story online before you've told it in real life to people that actually know you. Flesh it out first with wise counsel.

What makes it harder to speak about your story with some-one who really knows you—especially when you are talking to unbelievers—is this: to tell your story about how Jesus has changed you is to have to live up to God changing you—to stay changed. That's the harder thing—but it might actually end up being the more fruitful thing. Telling a story to an un-believer in that kind of way can come off as more authentic, because it's not just audible or readable. It's also practical.

I think the assumption by people in our culture is often that Christians don't struggle—that Christians just have a very easy life. You know how this assumption goes: our kids are well behaved, our marriages are all great, and we don't struggle with pornography or lust or greed or all these other things that drag people down, and that in fact do drag Christians down too sometimes. And so actually to tell the stories of what happened yesterday and the stories of what happened last week allows us to speak more honestly and authentically about our experience of everyday life and its struggles. "I didn't trust God about this, but I trust him now." Faith is practical and renewed every day. We are trusting God on Tuesday, Wednesday, and Thursday in the same way that we trusted him ten years ago when we got on our knees for the first time and said, "God, forgive me."

Telling stories gets across the fact that the gospel doesn't just save you but changes you daily.

People need to be able to see that the gospel works. They don't just want to hear "Jesus is good"; they want to see if his goodness has reached down into how we live our lives. They need to know that God can change them. That is what every Christian story can demonstrate. *Now I'm different.* Whether that's different than ten years ago or different than this morn-ing, it gives people real hope.

BEING VULNERABLE

If you want to teach yourself the habit of telling your story, a good way to begin is by telling it to other Christians.

Every week in my church small group two people volunteer to share their stories through photos before we begin our Bible study, so that we can get to know each other. One of my friends told the story of her divorce. She is only 27, so it was surprising to the majority of the group to know that about her.

Her being willing to share her story allowed us to learn something about her life that none of us knew. We wouldn't have found that out just by going on Facebook or Twitter. But we know that now.

Ask yourself: Do my Christian friends even know my story? Do the people in my local community know what I've been through—what God has saved me from?

It's understandable if they don't, because we all have a vulnerability and an intimacy problem. We are often afraid to free ourselves from our own constrictions and be honest with each other. Why? Two reasons: fear, and shame.

I understand fear. It is a very human thing. But fear is a liar. Fear tells us that this person's opinion matters more than an unbeliever's salvation or a believer's edification.

I understand shame, too. To relive stories might reignite the feelings of shame that those situations brought—whether it was promiscuity, whether it was porn addiction, whether it was something as small as having been afraid to talk about Jesus in school all those years. It's painful to relive such stories and the shame of denying God.

But we have to recognize that the gospel takes our fear and our shame away. When Jesus was on the cross—naked, bloodied, and beaten—he took the shame that you deserve, and he erased the one thing truly worth fearing, which is the rejection and the wrath of God. You don't have to carry that fear and shame: Jesus carried it already. You're forgiven.

Fear and shame began in the Garden of Eden, in Genesis 3. As soon as Adam and Eve ate the fruit, they hid from God, and they were ashamed. That's what we, too, are experiencing on the daily. Sin has made us want to hide: to keep our loincloths over ourselves and our stories and our past, and even over our current struggles. So we try to project a false kind of wholeness. But the more intimate we are with God—the more we enjoy all that we are and have in Jesus—the more willing we are to be intimate and vulnerable with each other.

In the end it all depends upon the heart. If I'm not telling my story just because I didn't think about it, that's fine, but I have to ask the question: Why haven't I thought about it? If it's because of fear or shame, then I need to deal with that. On the opposite side, it is possible to tell our stories out of pride. We can want to be seen and applauded and esteemed: "*Look at them. They found Jesus. They overcame.*"

So there needs to be a process of looking at our hearts and trying to understand ourselves. Ask the Holy Spirit to reveal your heart's motives. Read the Bible, which is like a two-edged sword (Hebrews 4 v 12) and can bring to your mind the ways in which you are not acting like Jesus. Then with his help you will change, and that will be another part of your story.

"THAT'S NOT MY STORY"

I was at Harvard University once to tell my story about sexuality, and I had a conversation with this guy who asked me, "What are you here for?" He knew why I was there, but that's what he said. And I replied, "I'm just telling my story."

Then he said, "Do you think that your story is supposed to be everybody else's story?" Which is a good question. And I said, "Not necessarily."

My story is my story, and it is true; but my story ultimately is not authoritative. Yet my story is undergirded by an authoritative reality, which is that Christ has died for sinners like me, and that sinners like me are to repent and believe in him.

If we use our stories to point to the authority of God and his Scriptures, then our stories actually have more power than other stories that have no authority. Your story may seem to be just merely experience, but when it's undergirded by truth, it has an immense amount of power. Sharing your story about God's grace in your life may seem to be a small thing, but remember, there is truth wrapped up in it—truth which can change everything because it is powerful to save (Romans 1 v 16).

So, when people say to me, "That's your experience. That's not mine," I don't want to allow that to be the end of the conversation. I try to follow their lead: "Tell me your experience." Then I listen to them and, as led by the Holy Spirit, I try to point their experience to the truth.

Let's say they say, "That's not my experience. I don't have any struggles like that."

I'll answer, "Why not? Why do you think that? You don't have any hardships at all?"

"Well, yeah. Yeah, I do."

"Why do you think that is?"

"I don't know why."

And then I can say, "Well, have you ever heard about sin and how it has impacted the way the world is shaped and formed?"

It's finding ways to use the person's own pushback to actually continue the conversation. I know it takes some wisdom to do this. That's why, when I'm talking to people, I'm praying the entire time, because I want the Holy Spirit to be there.

The way somebody responds to my story reveals what their idols are, and what they think about God and life and the gospel. And therefore I see my story really as a first step toward getting deeper. If I'm in a conversation with you, my story is not enough. We need to get to *your* heart issues and *your* belief system. I want to get beyond me and talk to your heart.

To think that this one conversation will be enough to bring someone to Christ is silly. Do we have hope for it? Do we pray for it? Yes. But we don't set ourselves up to think that it is solely our words or our experiences that will change a person's heart.

We tell our stories because it's God's word that pierces the heart. It's his same word that has pierced our own hearts and changed us from within.

> *For God, who said, "Let light shine out of darkness," has shone in our hearts to give the light of the knowledge of the glory of God in the face of Jesus Christ.*
> *(2 Corinthians 4 v 6)*

By his grace, now I'm different. That's a beautiful story. It declares glory to all who will listen. And just think how our sovereign, saving God may use it.

AFTERWORD

TRILLIA NEWBELL

Beautifully Distinct is a resource for personal use but could also be read within the context of a book study. Here are some questions you might use to guide a conversation or for self-reflection.

- What did you find surprising in the book or in a specific chapter?
- What was the biggest challenge?
- What was the greatest comfort?
- How might you apply the various topics to your life?
- What is one area you can begin praying for as a result of your reading?
- We've only scratched the surface of many of these topics. Are there any that you hope to dive further into?
- What is one text of Scripture from each chapter that you could meditate on this week?
- How can these topics assist you in engaging the world around you?

My hope is that you and I will walk boldly in the world, knowing that Jesus is with us and that God is for us. We can be a light to a dark world. None of us will do this perfectly; but knowing we will walk imperfectly enables us to also walk humbly. That is my prayer for you and for me.

ENDNOTES

1. MOVIES: SPEAKING OUR CULTURE'S LANGUAGE

[1] Josh Larsen, *Movies Are Prayers: How Films Voice Our Deepest Longings* (IVP, 2017).

3. SEX AND OUR BODIES

[1] Jeff Shapiro, "Percentage of Christians, Americans Who Have Read 'Fifty Shades of Grey' the Same," www.christianpost.com/news/percentage-of-christians-americans-who-have-read-fifty-shades-of-grey-the-same-97353 (accessed Dec. 16 2019).

[2] "Report of the APA Task Force on the Sexualization of Girls" (American Psychological Association, 2007).

[3] Eileen Kennedy Moore, "Teen Sexting in Perspective," www.psychologytoday.com/gb/blog/growing-friendships/201603/teen-sexting-in-perspective (accessed Nov. 22 2019).

[4] Wendy Shalit, "The Private Self(ie)," www.time.com/3269540/celebrity-photo-hack-selfies-jennifer-lawrence-modesty (accessed Nov. 22 2019).

[5] Robert Covolo, "The Biblical Meaning of Clothing," www.christianitytoday.com/ct/2015/july-august/biblical-meaning-of-clothing.html (accessed Nov. 22 2019).

5. THE VALUE OF LITERATURE

[1] Interview on www.thegospelcoalition.org, Jun. 2 2007.

7. LOVING THE STRANGER, LOVING THE IMMIGRANT

[1] Linda Bloom, "Small Churches Play Big Role for Refugees in Italy," www.umnews.org/en/news/small-churches-play-big-role-for-refugees-in-italy (accessed Oct. 18 2019).

[2] Katy Fallon, "Yazidis Seek Church Asylum as Europe's Empathy for Refugees Wanes," www.aljazeera.com/indepth/features/yazidis-seek-church-asylum-europe-empathy-refugees-wanes-18082822 1815711.html (accessed Oct. 18 2019).

[3] Melissa Vida, "How a Brussels Church Became a Home for Latin American Refugees," www.americamagazine.org/politics-society/2019/06/04/how-brussels-church-became-home-latin-american-refugees (accessed Oct. 18 2019).

[4] Churches' Commission for Migrants and Conference of European Churches, "Christmas Statement," www.oikoumene.org/en/resources/documents/other-ecumenical-bodies/christmas-statement (accessed Dec. 4 2018).

8. CONVERSATIONS ON RACE

[1] "Status and Trends in the Education of Racial and Ethnic Groups 2018" (National Center of Education Statistics, U.S. Dept of Education), www.nces.ed.gov/pubs2019/2019038.pdf (accessed Sep. 27 2019).

2   CNN, "A Look at Race Relations Through a Child's Eyes," www.youtube.com/watch?v=GPVNJgfDwpw (accessed Mar. 13 2017).

3   Christopher Ingraham, "Three Quarters of Whites Don't Have Any Non-White Friends," www.washingtonpost.com/news/wonk/wp/2014/08/25/three-quarters-of-whites-dont-have-any-non-white-friends/?utm_term=.2fb20a7c34ec (accessed Mar. 13 2017).

4   Emily Swanson, "Do Most White Americans Really Only Have White Friends? Let's Take a Closer Look," www.huffingtonpost.com/2014/09/03/black-white-friends-poll_n_5759464.html (accessed Mar. 13 2017).

9. SURFING THE SOCIAL-MEDIA WAVE

1   "Social Media 'Likes' Impact Teens' Brains and Behavior," www.psychologicalscience.org/news/releases/social-media-likes-impact-teens-brains-and-behavior.html (accessed May 21 2016).

2   Hartley-Parkinson, "You Can't Hug a Facebook Friend," www.dailymail.co.uk/sciencetech/article-2026086/Facebook-Young-people-spend-time-online-theyre-lonely-elderly.html (accessed Nov. 22 2019).

3   As above.

4   Sandra Bond Chapman, "Is Your Brain Being Wired by Technology?" blogs.wsj.com/drivers-seat/2012/12/05/two-hands-on-the-smartphone-industry-looks-at-driver-distraction (accessed Oct. 18 2012).

5   These statistics come from Albert Mohler, "The Scandal of Biblical Illiteracy: It's Our Problem," www.albertmohler.com/2016/01/20/the-scandal-of-bibli-cal-illiteracy-its-our-problem-4 (accessed Jan. 20 2016).

10. WHAT WE SAY ABOUT BEAUTY

[1]   I developed these ideas more fully in session 6 of my Bible-study series, *1 Peter: A Living Hope in Christ* (LifeWay, 2016).

CONTRIBUTORS

TRILLIA NEWBELL is the author of *If God is For Us, God's Very Good Idea,* and *Sacred Endurance.* She is the Director of Community Outreach for the Ethics & Religious Liberty Commission of the SBC.

ALISSA WILKINSON is a film critic, writer, and an associate professor at The King's College in New York City, where she teaches criticism and cultural theory.

KAREN SWALLOW PRIOR is the author of *Booked* and *On Reading Well,* and Research Professor of English and Christianity & Culture at Southeastern Baptist Theological Seminary. She writes on literature, culture, ethics, and ideas.

CATHERINE PARKS is the author of four books, including *Real, Empowered,* and *Strong.* She enjoys helping women connect around studying the Bible and prayer.

KELLY NEEDHAM is a blogger and the author of *Friendish.* She has previously been on staff at two different churches, serving in youth, college, and women's ministry.

DANNAH GRESH is a writer and speaker, and the founder of True Girl, a live event for tweens and moms. Her books include *And the Bride Wore White* and *Lies Girls Believe.*

CHELSEA PATTERSON SOBOLIK is a Policy Director at the Ethics & Religious Liberty Commission, and the author of *Longing for Motherhood: Finding Hope in the Midst of Childlessness.*

JACKIE HILL PERRY is a writer, poet, and artist. She is the author of *Gay Girl, Good God* and *Jude: Contending For the Faith in Today's Culture.*

COURTNEY REISSIG is a writer and speaker. She is involved in women's ministry and is the author of *Teach Me to Feel* and *Glory in the Ordinary.*

JENNY YANG is SVP of Advocacy and Policy at World Relief. She is co-author of *Welcoming the Stranger* and serves as Chair of the Refugee Council USA Africa Work Group.

NATASHA SISTRUNK ROBINSON is the author of *Mentor for Life* and *Sojourner's Truth.* She is a leadership, diversity, and mentoring coach; speaker; and Bible teacher.

LILLY PARK is Assistant Professor of Biblical Counseling at the Southern Baptist Theological Seminary.

LINDSAY NICOLET is Managing Editor of Content at the Ethics & Religious Liberty Commission, where she manages the day-to-day content of ERLC.com.

ERIN DAVIS loves to see women of all ages run to the deep well of God's word. She is the author of many books and Bible studies for women and teens.

JEN WILKIN is an author and Bible teacher, and Executive Director of Next Gen Ministries at The Village Church, Texas. Her books include *Women of the Word, None Like Him,* and *In His Image.*

COMPANY

BIBLICAL | RELEVANT | ACCESSIBLE

At The Good Book Company, we are dedicated to helping Christians and local churches grow. We believe that God's growth process always starts with hearing clearly what he has said to us through his timeless word—the Bible.

Ever since we opened our doors in 1991, we have been striving to produce Bible-based resources that bring glory to God. We have grown to become an international provider of user-friendly resources to the Christian community, with believers of all backgrounds and denominations using our books, Bible studies, devotionals, evangelistic resources, and DVD-based courses.

We want to equip ordinary Christians to live for Christ day by day, and churches to grow in their knowledge of God, their love for one another, and the effectiveness of their outreach.

Call us for a discussion of your needs or visit one of our local websites for more information on the resources and services we provide.

Your friends at The Good Book Company

thegoodbook.com | thegoodbook.co.uk
thegoodbook.com.au | thegoodbook.co.nz
thegoodbook.co.in